Need

Information Sources in
Patents

Guides to Information Sources

A series under the General Editorship of
D. J. Foskett, MA, FLA
and
M. W. Hill, MA, BSc, MRIC

This series was known previously as 'Butterworths Guides to Information Sources'.

Other titles available include:

Information Sources in Sport and Leisure
edited by Michele Shoebridge

Information Sources for the Press and Broadcast Media
edited by Selwyn Eagle

Information Sources in the Medical Sciences (Fourth edition)
edited by L.T. Morton and S. Godbolt

Information Sources in Information Technology
edited by David Haynes

Information Sources in Grey Literature (Second edition)
by C.P. Auger

Information Sources in Pharmaceuticals
edited by W.R. Pickering

Information Sources in Metallic Materials
edited by M.N. Patten

Information Sources in the Earth Sciences (Second edition)
edited by David N. Wood, Joan E. Hardy and Anthony P. Harvey

Information Sources in Cartography
edited by C.R. Perkins and R.B. Barry

Information Sources in Polymers and Plastics
edited by R.T. Adkins

Information Sources in Science and Technology (Second edition)
edited by C.C. Parker and R.V. Turley

Information Sources in Physics (Second edition)
edited by Dennis Shaw

Information Sources in Economics (Second edition)
edited by John Fletcher

Information Sources in the Life Sciences (Third edition)
edited by H.V. Wyatt

Information Sources in Engineering (Second edition)
edited by L.J. Anthony

Information Sources in
Patents

Edited by
C.P. Auger

Bowker-Saur

London • Melbourne • Munich • New York

British Library Cataloguing in Publication Data
A catalogue record for this book is available from the
British Library

Library of Congress Cataloging-in-Publication Data
A catalog record for this book is available from the Library of
Congress

Bowker-Saur is part of the Professional Division of
Reed International Books, 60 Grosvenor Street, London W1X 9DA

Cover design by Calverts Press
Printed on acid-free paper
Typeset by SunSetters
Printed and bound in Great Britain by Antony Rowe Ltd, Chippenham,
Wiltshire

Series editors' foreword

As is obvious, any human being, faced with solving a problem or with understanding a task, reacts by thinking, by applying judgement and by seeking information. The first two involve using information from the most readily available source, namely one's memory, though searching this and retrieving what is wanted may be conducted below the level of consciousness. If this source does not provide all that is needed then the information searcher may turn to all or any of three external sources: observation (which can consist simply of 'going and looking' or can involve understanding sophisticated research); other people, who may be close colleagues or distant experts; and stores of recorded information, for example a local filing system or an electronic databank held on a computer network or even a book or journal in a national library.

The order (observation; other people; recorded information), is not significant though it is often a common sequence. Certainly it is not intended to impute an order of importance. Which of the three or what combination of them one uses depends on a number of factors including the nature of the problem and one's personal circumstances. Suffice to say that all three have their place and all three are used by every literate person.

Nowadays the amount of information in any field, even if one can exclude that which has been superseded, is so large that no human being or small group of people can hope to know it all. Thus, company information systems, for example, get bigger and bigger even when there are efficient means of discarding unwanted and out-of-date information. Managing these systems is a complex and full time task.

Many factors contribute to the huge information growth and overload. Throughout the world, large amounts of research continue to be undertaken and their results published for others to use or follow up. New data pours out of the financial markets. Governments keep passing new legislation. The law courts keep generating new rulings. Each organization and everyone in it of any significance, it seems, is in the business of generating new information. Most of it is recorded and much of it is published.

Although there is a growing tendency to record information in electronic media and to leave it there for distribution via electronic networks of one sort or another, the traditional media are still in use. Even tablets of stone are still used in appropriate circumstances but, of course, it is paper that predominates. The electronic age has not yet led to any reduction in the amount of printed material being published.

The range of types of published or publicly available information sources is considerable. It includes collections of letters, monographs, reports, pamphlets, newspapers and other periodicals, patent specifications, standards, trade literature including both manufacturers' product specifications and service companies' descriptions of their services, user manuals, laws, bye-laws, regulations and all the great wealth of leaflets poured out by official, semi-official and private organizations to guide the public. Then there are all those publications that present their information in other than verbal form; maps; graphs; music scores photographs; moving pictures; sound recordings; videos. Nor, although their main content is not published information, should one forget as sources of information collections of artefacts.

In an attempt to make some of the more frequently needed information more easily accessible, these sources of primary information are supplemented with the well-known range of tertiary publications, and text books, data books, reviews and encyclopaedias.

To find the information source one needs, another range of publications has come into being. to find experts or organizations or products there are directories, masses of them, so many that directories of directories are published. To find a required publication there are library catalogues, publishers' lists, indexes and abstracting services, again a great many of them.

For librarians and information specialists in the industrialized countries, access to abstracting services is now normally achieved on-line, i.e from a computer terminal over the telephone lines to remote computer-base database host. Since 1960 the use of libraries by information and even document seekers has changed considerably and can be expected to change further as the British Library study *Information 2000* indicates. More and more primary information is being stored electronically and more and more copies of printed documents are supplied via telephone or data networks. Sets of newspapers or other major publications can be acquired on optical discs for use in-house. Scientists in different universities, perhaps working on a common project, are sharing their results via the medium of electronic bulletin boards. The use of electronic messaging systems for disseminating information is now commonplace. Thus the combination of computer technology with telecommunications engineering is offering new ways of accessing and communicating information. Nevertheless, the old ways continue to be important and will remain so for many years yet.

The huge wealth of sources of information, the great range of resources, of means of identifying them and of accessing what is wanted increase the need for well aimed guides. Not all sources are of equal value even when only those well focused on the required topic are considered. The way new journals proliferate whenever a new major topic is established, many it seems just trying to 'climb on the bandwagon' and as a consequence substantially duplicating each other, illustrates this. Even in an established field the tendency of scientists, for example, to have a definite 'pecking order' for selecting journals in which to publish their research is well known. Some journals submit offered articles to referees; some others publish anything they can get. Similar considerations apply to other publications. The degree of reliance that can be placed on reports in different newspapers is an illustration. Nor is accuracy the only measure of quality. Another is the depth to which an account of a given topic goes.

The aim of this series *Guides to Information Sources*, is to give within each broad subject field (chemistry, architecture, politics, cartography etc.) an account of the types of external information source that exist and of the more important individual sources set in the context of the subject itself. Individual chapters are written by experts, each of whom specializes in the field he/she is describing, and give a view based on experience of finding and using the most appropriate sources. The volumes are intended to be readable by other experts and information seekers working outside their normal field. They are intended to help librarians concerned with problems of relevance and quality in stock selection.

Since not only the sources but also the needs and interests of users vary from one subject to another, each editor is given a free hand to produce the guide which is appropriate for his/her subject. We, the series editors, believe that this volume does just that.

Douglas Foskett
Michael Hill

Contents

Preface

Some forty years ago, as a very junior assistant on the staff of Birmingham Public Libraries, I was one day despatched to the Commercial Library for a period of relief duty to cover for an absent colleague. The Commercial Library was then housed in a separate building in the heart of Birmingham's banking quarter, and on going there I had naively expected that I would be dealing with business publications such as financial journals, trade directories and collections of statistics.

My first job on arrival was the replacing, on narrow shelves reachable only by cast iron spiral staircases, of a considerable pile of unfamiliar bound volumes which were both bulky to handle and heavy to lift. The contents of these weighty tomes turned out to be sequences of United States patent specifications, beautifully covered in bookbinders' best-quality cream-coloured linen.

From that day onwards I never had the slightest doubt that patents were a special form of literature - vast in quantity, awkward to handle, lovingly preserved, and belonging both to the world of business and to the world of science and technology.

Nowadays the City of Birmingham has chosen to house its patents collection on the science and technology floor of the new reference library, and the intervening years have given me ample time to reflect on its true nature and purpose.

The present work attempts to explore the origins of patent systems, how they work today, and why despite all the apparent difficulties they remain more than ever a most important source for those whose responsibility it is to search for scientific, technical and commercial information.

The bulk of the text is based on my own experience with patents in public libraries, in research and development laboratories, and in manufacturing industry; it is inspired by the earlier title 'Mainly on Patents', and is greatly reinforced by contributions from experts in specialist areas.

To the writers of these chapters, and to the many other people who have assisted by providing material and supplying helpful comments, I extend my grateful thanks.

CPA

CHAPTER ONE

The purpose of patents

Introduction

The aim of the present work is to indicate how the patent system originated, how it works today, and why, despite all the apparent difficulties, it remains more than ever a most important source for those whose responsibility it is to search for technical information. Traditionally when embarking on new projects, especially those in research and development, the first step is to conduct a thorough literature survey to establish both the prior art and the state of the art. Patents of course do feature in such surveys, but quite frequently they are treated as a separate resource, and the subject of a separate investigation, only to be examined closely if the more traditional types of publication fail to yield the desired data.

Thus, by looking in detail at how a patent is drawn up, how it is presented and the way in which it seeks to disclose and at the same time protect ideas, it is hoped that the source will become more accessible, that people will learn to lose their misgivings and reservations about it, and that they will come to realize that to exploit it fully requires a proper appreciation of its nature and purpose.

The statement is often made that patents constitute a vast storehouse of information on scientific and technical topics, about 80% of which is not published in any other form. By its very nature (for the word 'patent' comes from the Latin *patere*, to lie open) patent literature is, or ought to be, available to all who care to read and study it, and yet patents constitute a category of publication regarded by many as difficult to understand and difficult to relate to other forms of publication, such as books, journals, papers and reports.

That it should be regarded as hard to understand leads to a further paradox, for the principles behind the description contained in a typical specification are embodied in the concept that anyone skilled in the art should be able to follow and reproduce the invention disclosed. With patience and perseverance, and disregarding for a moment the question of the definition of a person skilled in the art, this is undoubtedly true, but patent specifications are not noted for their lucidity, and scientists and engineers frequently express the view that they prefer more assimilable information, not to say more user-friendly accounts of technical advances and developments.

Quite rightly, patents ought to be seen as a prime source of technical information, to be eagerly studied and acted upon – they are rich in detail, explicit sometimes to the point of pedantry, and more often than not accompanied by very detailed drawings and diagrams. The general experience of librarians and information specialists indicates, however, that patents are regarded as the information source of last resort – the classic case where the seeker after technical detail can be taken to the water but cannot be induced to drink. There are many reasons for a widespread prejudice against the medium, which is a pity, for the basic assertion is assuredly true – patents do represent a reservoir of information both current and historical, which is unparalleled in scope, depth and detail.

A number of studies have shown that many informed users regard patents as a prime source of technical information, in some cases the most important source. For example a paper by Wyatt *et al.*[1] based on a report prepared for AREPIT (Association de Recherche Economique en Propriétés Intéllectuelles et Transfers Techniques, Paris) describes a study concerned with the role of patenting in multinational corporations' (MNCs) strategies for growth. Results are based on responses to questionnaires received from the patenting departments of 80 MNCs (out of a target of 400), and the authors conclude that 'patents are a useful source of qualitative and quantitative information on technological change (and that) patents appear to be widely used as a source of technical information'.

The composition of the sectors used in the analysis was:

1.   Pharmaceuticals
2.   Other chemicals
3.   Electrical engineering and electronics
4.   Mechanical engineering
5.   Automobiles
6.   Resource-based (metals, oil refining, minerals, petroleum).

Patents are a unique source of information, and failure to include them in literature searches can cost an organization dear. Quite separately from their legal significance, which is discussed elsewhere in this volume, patents constitute a systematic body of scientific and technical literature which also has the virtue of imparting commercial intelligence to those who seek it out. Many statements have been made about the benefits of patents as a source of information, and the generally agreed but by no means exhaustive list runs as follows:

● Patents embrace practically every area of applied science and technology, and inventions range from simple mechanisms to complex chemical compounds.

● Patents represent solutions to problems, for inventors build on the inventions of those already in the field.

● Patents are highly detailed, containing meticulous descriptions frequently accompanied by detailed drawings and diagrams.

● Patents have a historical significance, and they are often used in tracing the development of specific concepts, technologies and processes.

● Patents are a source of information about people, in that they identify experts in a particular area and can be used to identify research and development teams in large organizations.

● Patents yield commercial information because specifications can reveal which companies are active in a particular market over a particular period.

As documents, patent specifications are subject to exacting bibliographical control, classified in great detail according to regularly updated subject schemes, and readily searchable via online databases using a variety of search categories, including patent number, classification number, inventor, company, and by broad or narrow subject concepts. In fact patents worldwide represent an extremely well organized, accessible collection of literature, and for those who make the attempt to acquire familiarity with it, the rewards well repay the effort.

The question of familiarity is forcefully emphasized by Stephenson,[2] who in a study of the usage of Newcastle Patents Library noted that 'a missing link in the chain of effective patent information use is the dynamic influence of a lively exploiter being or acting as a patent information officer, who can position himself between the information and the potential user'.

With these preliminary thoughts in mind, it is necessary to start at the beginning and reflect to some degree on why a system of patents grew up in the first place.

Definitions

Patents are a form of intellectual property, and intellectual property itself has been defined in the treaty establishing the World Intellectual Property Organization (WIPO), signed in Stockholm in 1968, as 'all legal rights resulting from intellectual activity in the industrial, literary or artistic fields'. The present work is primarily concerned with information arising from the exercise of those rights in industry and commerce, as distinct from the literary and artistic aspects, whilst acknowledging at the same time that there is certainly no clear boundary between the arts and commerce.

To enlarge on the WIPO definition, intellectual property is 'a form of intangible property created largely through the application of the intellect to technical or commercial matters'. Since it is a form of property, it has an owner or a proprietor, with the assumption that as property it also has some value. The property is intangible, since although the documents which represent the various forms of intellectual property are themselves tangible, it is the intellectual content of the documents to which the value attaches.

In order to put matters in context, it is necessary to consider briefly the principal forms which intellectual property can take, especially in order to appreciate the alternatives to patents which are available, and which in some cases may be a more appropriate form of protection.

Firstly, patents themselves: a patent is a statutory protection for a term of years (now rarely exceeding 20) for a technical concept, defined in most modern systems by a statement known as a claim. Such a concept can be a process, which can encompass a new use of an old material, or a device and the use of that device. The key feature of a patent is that the idea which it embodies must be disclosed early on in its life, and that in return for the disclosure someone obtains a limited monopoly. The degree of protection which a patent affords depends on the jurisdiction under which it is granted, and because it has to be drafted as a legal document in order to obtain protection for the concept, by comparing a tangible technical development such as a machine with a conceptual definition, it does not make for easy reading as a source of technical information. Patents offer a form of objective protection, and if an infringer is found it is irrelevant as to how that infringer developed his own particular technology.

Another form of intellectual property is the industrial design, where the intention is to protect appearance. Design registration is treated as a branch of copyright in some countries, whilst in others such as the USA it is given more of the aspects of patents. As with patents, registered designs offer objective protection, and if an infringer is found it is irrelevant how he came to arrive at his own design.

A further form of intellectual property is copyright, which, briefly stated, is the concept that the concrete expression of an author or creator is protectable against reproduction of that expression by others. The protection in this case is subjective, in that for there to be a misuse of copyright there must be an act of copying. Copyright in most countries does not require any registration procedure.

Whereas patents, registered designs and copyright offer protection through the exercise of statutory rights, there is another form of intellectual property important to the information searcher, which, at least in the United Kingdom, is a matter of common law, namely trade secrets and know–how. Trade secrets include patentable inventions such as chemical processes in which the final product does not reveal the method of manufacture, a consideration which explains why many organizations choose not to disclose the details. Trade secrets also embrace unpatentable concepts not easily derivable by a competitor, such as the formula for a consumer product such as a soft drink.

Know-how is a concept difficult to separate satisfactorily from trade secrets, but its distinguishing feature is a skill in solving problems. Trade secrets and know–how are of great interest to the seeker after information, but they generally remain inaccessible because they are not part of an openly available literature.

The final form of intellectual property to be considered here is the trademark, an identifiable word or symbol associated with certain goods, or, more recently in Great Britain, with services. A trademark is an aspect of the larger topic of goodwill, and at least in Great Britain it need not be a registered protection, since the concept of unregistered trademarks still exists.

A final term in need of definition or at least clarification, is industrial property as distinct from intellectual property. The latter term as has been seen, is very wide in scope and covers all forms of property created largely through the application of the intellect.

Industrial property is a much narrower concept, and normally relates to intellectual property which is subject to some form of registration procedure, notably patents, trademarks and designs, although as already noted, trademarks need not be registered and some legislations provide for the registration of copyright. One of the characteristics of industrial property, arising of course from the act of registration, is that the items it encompasses can be numbered in recognizable sequences, thus providing both a unique identifier and the basis for compiling statistics. Unregistered intellectual property on the other hand has to be identified and accounted for by other means.

Brief history

In Great Britain the idea of patents grew out of the concept of a protected industry, and the word patent itself arises from the expression 'letters patent', that is to say a writing issued by or in the name of the sovereign, addressed to all subjects and with the Great Seal pendent at the bottom of the document, usually a sheet of parchment, so that it could be read without breaking the seal. A 15th century reference to the term's original meaning is to be found in the Paston Letters (PL 219): 'Sir, forasmuch as the King has granted by these letters patent the wardship... of the lands of T. Fatsolf during his nonage...'.

Letters patent are still used in Great Britain, for example, to confer peerages and appoint judges, but are no longer used to grant patents for invention under the current Patents Act. Before 1878 letters patent for inventions were engrossed on parchment and bore the Great Seal in wax. Subsequently paper was used and a wafer seal of the Patent Office replaced the Great Seal, but the wording of the letters patent document (not to be confused with the printed specification) still had the feel of another, more leisurely age, with a command from the Queen to her subjects to refrain from infringing the patent under pain of royal displeasure. Nowadays a more pragmatic approach is adopted, and the patentee simply gets a certificate from the Patent Office.

An early example of industrial rights conferred under the Royal Prerogative was the grant by Henry VI, in 1449, of protection for a method of making coloured glass. Although monopolies were a convenient way of raising money, the emphasis was on protection rather than innovation, and in 1601 a proclamation was issued that such monopolies could be challenged. It was also necessary to take measures against infringers, and in 1602 Edward Darcy, holder of a patent on making playing cards, brought an action against a haberdasher for infringing the patent. Unfortunately for Darcy the outcome was that the patent was held to be invalid. Proclamations continued to be issued until 1624, when the first British statute on patent law came into force, the so–called Statute of Monopolies. The statute granted monopolies of 14 years, a period based on the time it took to train two generations of apprentices.

In other countries the linguistic equivalents of letters patent came from deeds and somewhat similar concepts, and a browse through a file of patent documents from around the world will yield a rich harvest of embellishments, in the form of coloured ribbons, decorative seals and elaborate scripts.

Rights given by a patent do not include the right to practise the invention, but simply to exclude others from doing so, because the patentee's freedom may be restricted by legislation or regulations unconnected with patents, or of course by the existence of other patents.

The 18th century witnessed an acceleration in the granting of patents, and the surge of inventiveness from that time on can be traced in the comprehensive synopsis compiled by Westcott and Spratt[3], which charts developments in mechanical and electrical engineering in all parts of the world, from the earliest times to 1958. The synopsis cites many patents of historical significance, highlighting inventions which have gone on to become household names, including James Watt's first patent (1769), the Stirling engine (1816), the Colt revolver (1835), the Diesel engine (1892) and many, many more.

The Industrial Revolution in particular was a period of growth in the granting of patents and the painstaking study by Dutton[4] notes that no single industry was especially significant in terms of taking out patent protection. In an analysis of the direction of patents activity ranked by process, the top five (out of a total of 17 101 patents appearing during the period 1750–1851) were:

Rank	Process	Patents	Percentage
1	Steam	984	5.75
2	Hydraulics	750	4.38
3	Spinning	715	4.18
4	Fuel	714	4.17
5	Carriages	586	3.42

The position of steam at the top of the table is not surprising given its importance as the driving force of the Industrial Revolution, but the actual percentage seems surprisingly small. The theme of steam is further explored by Davenport[5], in his study of James Watt and the patent system, in which he provides an introduction to the history of patents by relating the story of Watt (1736–1819) in terms of his encounters with the patent system of the day. Davenport points out that whilst few inventors had involved themselves in the patent system, Watt himself had made a number of suggestions for changing the patent law.

Changes there certainly were, as in subsequent years parliament began from time to time to devote some attention to patents. Thus the year 1835 saw the first piece of legislation since the Statute of Monopolies, with an act which provided for some small changes, one of which was the ability of patentees to amend their specifications for the purpose of removing small errors. In 1852, the Patent Law Amendment Act met many of the wishes of a considerable lobby of reformers: the administration of the patent system was simplified, with the setting up of the Patent Office to grant a single patent to cover the whole of the United Kingdom, instead of separate patents for England, Scotland and Ireland; inventions were to be protected from the time of application, and proposals were announced for an index of patents.

Further modifications occurred in 1883, when the Act of that year required specifications to contain at least one claim; in addition a complete specification had to be filed before the patent was granted. However, throughout the 19th century patents were granted in the United Kingdom without anything more than a purely formal examination, and only in 1902 did a further act provide for examination for novelty.

In 1919, the term of a patent was increased from 14 to 16 years, and 30 years later the 1949 Patents Act came on to the statute book, mainly as a codification of the gradual changes in the law which had resulted from decisions by the courts. Indeed, apart from the restoration of protection for chemical substances (a measure abandoned in 1919), the act contained little that was really new.

The same could not be said of the 1977 Patents Act, which introduced major changes into British patent law. Firstly, the act was designed to update and improve the existing domestic law, and secondly it was drafted to enable United Kingdom and European patent laws to coexist, with the London Patent Office operating side by side with the European Patent Office in Munich. The consequences of this coexistence and its effect on the number of applications filed in London, will be examined later.

The Patents Act 1977 remains the principal source of law relating to United Kingdom patents, notwithstanding the Copyright, Designs and Patents Act of 1988, which is mainly concerned with copyright law. The 1988 Act does, however, make a number of changes to law and practice in the patent area, the underlying ideas for which were first aired in two widely discussed Government papers. These were the 1983 green paper[6] '*Intellectual Property Rights and Innovation*' and its successor, the white paper[7] '*Intellectual Property and Innovation*', published in 1986. The papers sought to stimulate discussion on ways of making the patent system user–friendly and more accessible, in order to encourage the exploitation of creative ideas.

Such sentiments were, in part, a recognition of the fact that many businessmen found patents 'intimidating', a view confirmed for example by the study[8] on the usage and usefulness of patent information for industries in the conurbation centred around Newcastle upon Tyne.

The main changes in patents introduced by the 1988 Act were:

● The ending of the Patent Agents' monopoly (see below).

● The empowerment of the Lord Chancellor to designate any county court as a patents county court, with the objective of providing a cheaper and speedier forum for disputes which do not justify seeking settlement through the expensive and often protracted High Court route.

● The provision of a solution to the problem of licences of right in respect of the last 4 years of patents, for pharmaceutical inventions patented before the 1977 Act.

The Paris Union

In parallel with the changes in patent law which took place in Great Britain and elsewhere during the 19th century, was the recognition that the laws of a country relating to industrial property were (and still are) generally concerned only with acts accomplished or committed within the country itself. Thus a patent became effective only in the country where it was granted, and it was not effective in other countries. To remedy this state of affairs, the owner of a patent who wanted protection in several countries had to obtain that protection in each of them separately.

It was therefore in order to guarantee the possibilities of obtaining protection in foreign countries for their own citizens, that in 1883 eleven countries (including Great Britain) established the International Union for the Protection of Industrial Property, by signing the Paris Convention for the Protection of Industrial Property. Since that time the number of states party to the convention has grown to 100, and the convention itself has been revised several times. The Paris Convention has proved to be one of the most successful and enduring acts of international cooperation ever put into effect. The convention's secretariat is furnished by the World Intellectual Property Organization (WIPO), and although the act of obtaining protection in individual countries has been affected by the subsequent appearance of the European patent, the convention's basic idea of 'right of priority' remains unchanged. This means that on the basis of a regular first application filed in one of the contracting states, the applicant may within a certain period of time (12 months for patents, less for trademarks and industrial designs) apply for protection in any of the other contracting states. These later applications will then be regarded as if they had been filed on the same day as the first application. In other words the later application will have priority over applications which may have been filed during the same period of time by other persons for the same invention.

One of the great practical advantages of this provision is that when an applicant desires protection for his invention in several countries, he is not required to present all his applications at the same time, but has 12 months at his disposal to decide in which countries he really wants protection, and to arrange the steps he must take to secure that protection. He also has time to consider the expense involved.

Under the convention, the first patent document to be published is called the basic patent; all the rest are called equivalents, and the group as a whole is called a family. The role of WIPO and other activities of an international character are discussed in Chapter 6.

Despite its enduring nature, however, it must be mentioned that the integrity of the Paris Union is under attack from a number of third-world countries, who are also contracting parties to the General Agreement on

Tariffs and Trade (GATT), and who wish to see a number of substantive changes with respect to patents.

The GATT is a large group of countries who believe that their best economic interests are served through a trading system based upon open markets and fair competition, secured through agreed multilateral rules and disciplines. The countries are bound together through a contract called, as noted above, the General Agreement on Tariffs and Trade – hence the term 'contracting parties'. Some countries regard patents as constituting unfair competition,[9] and want to see changes on the question of exclusions from patentable subject matter, especially for pharmaceutical, chemical and food products, and on the duration of the term of patent protection. The proposed changes are being stoutly resisted by the developed countries, and the outcome has still to be resolved.

The value of patents

Given the long pedigree of the present-day patent system, and bearing in mind that to many people the concept of a monopoly is anathema, it is not surprising that various theories have arisen as to the value of patents to society at large. The justifying arguments most frequently advanced fall into four main groups:

- Patents constitute a reward to the inventor in the form of an incentive.
- Patents embody natural justice by ensuring a fair reward to creative individuals.
- Patents are an important aspect of economic theory, in that it can be argued that they stimulate growth.
- Patents disclose information, the availability of which encourages the spread of inventions.

Looking more closely at each of these arguments, the natural justice thesis assumes that individuals have a natural right of property in their own ideas, a view which prevails on the continent, whilst the reward by monopoly idea argues that an inventor should be rewarded according to the usefulness of his invention by means of an exclusive privilege of limited duration. This thesis is a pragmatic recognition of the virtue of private reward.

The economic theory that patents stimulate growth argues that inventive activity can be associated with progress as well as private profit, and some exponents seek to establish a causal link between patents, invention and industrial development.

The information theory, based on an exchange of secrets by means of a disclosure agreement, is concerned largely with the dissemination of information about existing technology, which would otherwise remain hidden.

When one adds to the above theories Proudhon's dictum 'La propriété, c'est le vol', it is clear that there is plenty of scope for discussions about the pros and cons of the patent system, discussions which need not unduly detain the user of patents as a source of information, since his main task is to exploit the resources as he finds them. Perhaps the authoritative word on this aspect of patents should be left to the World Intellectual Property Organization, which says: 'Protection of industrial property is not of course an end in itself – it is a means to encourage creative activity, industrialization, investment and honest trade. All this is designed to contribute to more safety and comfort, less poverty, and more beauty in the lives of men'.

When considering the narrower aspect of the value of patents to information users it is important to note that, as will be discussed later, the format of a patent specification is carefully prescribed, with specific instructions as to the provision of a title, an abstract, a description, claims and drawings. What cannot be so closely defined is the level of quality with regard to the information content. Such an omission is in marked contrast to other forms of technical publication and disclosure, especially papers in journals and to meetings, where traditionally a double check is instituted through rules for presentation (style, citation of references, preparation of graphs, and so on) and an appraisal of excellence (achieved by the use of referees or members of an editorial board).

In consequence, a reader turning to a journal or the proceedings of a technical society can confidently expect certain standards to be maintained, which ensure that the ideas presented in the text and the illustrations are clear and consistent. Trivial contributions are screened out, pot-boilers are eliminated, and features which do not contribute positively to the reputation of the publishing bodies are referred back to the authors for further examination and revision.

A patent, on the other hand, is often an attempt to get something down in writing in order to establish priority. Specifications may have to be drafted before ideas have been fully developed, or before examples have been worked through to accumulate statistical or experimental data. The net result is a standard of quality in the information disclosed which can range from the very good to the frankly poor.

Naturally enough, once an inventor's first thoughts are published, the scrutiny they receive by the world at large will give an indication of their likelihood of proceeding to grant. It is possible to make an early assessment of the strength of an invention by taking into account the search report, with its list of relevant prior specifications and other material, and the initial reactions of other people working in the same field.

From the inventor's point of view it is a great disappointment to have to abandon an application; from the information searcher's point of view the merciless exposure of ideas is all grist to his mill, and he is well aware that the best place to look for the very latest technical information is in the unexamined applications, rather than the thinned ranks of granted patents.

A further limitation on the value of patents as a source of information lies in the fact that specifications may disclose very small modifications to well understood ideas and principles, and the effort of sifting out the nub of the inventive step may be greater than the benefit ultimately derived.

In short, patents are a valuable source of information, but in many cases that information is not readily yielded, and has to extracted in a manner akin to panning for gold. The problems which need to be recognized in order to capitalize on the great attractions of the currency of patents (in that they disclose information before it is reported elsewhere) and their exclusiveness (in that they reveal information not published in any other form) may be summarized as follows:

● Patents are segregated into separate collections often isolated from other literature.

● Patents are often written in a difficult form of language.

● Patents frequently disclose insufficient detail.

● Patents sometimes lack clarity and explicitness.

Such barriers are not inconsiderable, but are of course well worth overcoming in order to gain access to the information contained in patents – the various steps which can be taken to achieve these aims are examined in greater detail in the ensuing chapters.

References

1   Wyatt, S., Bertin, G. and Pavitt, K. (1985) Patents and multinational corporations: results from questionnaires. *World Patent Information*, **7**, (3), 196-212

2   Stephenson, J. (1982) The use of patent information in industry. *World Patent Information*, **4**, (4), 164-171

3   Westcott, G.F. (1960) *Synopsis of historical events: mechanical and electrical engineering*. Revised by H.P. Spratt. London: Her Majesty's Stationery Office

4   Dutton, H.I. (1984) *The patent system and inventive activity during the Industrial Revolution 1750-1852*. Manchester: University of Manchester Press

5   Davenport, A.N. (1990) *James Watt and the patent system*.

London: British Library, Science Reference and Information Service (SRIS)

6   *Intellectual property rights and innovation* (1983). London: Her Majesty's Stationery Office (Cmnd 9187)
7   *Intellectual property and innovation* (1986). London: Her Majesty's Stationery Office (Cmnd 9712)
8   Stephenson, J. and Riley, N.W. (1982) *The use of patent information in industry*. Boston Spa: British Library (Library and Information Research Report no 4)
9   Morris, G.D.L. (1989) GATT gets patent plea from India (enforcement to vary with country's level of development). *Chemical Week*, **145**, August 2, 14-15

CHAPTER TWO

The European patent

The European scene

It was been noted in the previous chapter that the laws of a country relating to industrial property are generally concerned only with acts accomplished or committed within that country itself. Thus a patent becomes effective only in the country where it is granted, and is not effective in other countries. A remedy is open to the owner of a patent who wants protection in several countries in that he can make separate applications in each of the countries of his choice, relying on the right of priority accorded by the provisions of the Paris Convention.

Unfortunately, obtaining protection for an invention in all the industrialized countries of the world where it is most likely to prove useful can be an expensive business. The costs of filing in Great Britain alone, albeit starting from a very modest application fee, can quickly increase to hundreds, or even thousands, of pounds, and this of course is on the basis of a relatively short document which is in the correct form from the outset. To include a group of a dozen or so overseas countries certainly means an expenditure of many thousands of pounds, plus various commitments on renewal fees.

These large costs were one of the reasons for the creation of the European patent, a form of protection for inventions available in the Contracting States to the European Patent Convention (EPC) (see list below). The Convention on the Grant of European Patents was concluded on 5 October 1973.

The European Patent Convention

The aim of the European Patent Convention (EPC) is to make the protection of inventions easier, cheaper and more reliable, by creating a simple European procedure for the grant of patents on the basis of a uniform body of substantive patent law. The contracting states are:

Austria	Liechtenstein
Belgium	Luxembourg
Denmark	Netherlands
France	Spain
Germany	Sweden
Greece	Switzerland
Italy	United Kingdom

This list needs to be compared with the make-up of the European Community (see Table 2.1):

Table 2.1 Contracting states in the European Community

1975	1989	1993
Belgium	Belgium	Austria*
Denmark	Denmark	Belgium
France	France	Cyprus*
Germany	Germany	Denmark
Ireland	Greece	France
Italy	Ireland	Germany
Luxembourg	Italy	Greece
Netherlands	Luxembourg	Ireland
United Kingdom	Netherlands	Italy
	Portugal	Luxembourg
	Spain	Malta*
	United Kingdom	Netherlands
		Portugal
		Spain
		Turkey*
		United Kindom

*decision on membership awaited

It will be noted that the list excludes two EEC countries (Ireland and Portugal) and includes four non-EEC countries (Austria, Liechtenstein, Sweden and Switzerland). The provisions of the EPC offer a procedure for securing what is usually termed a 'bundle' of patents. A single application is made, designating all or any of the contracting states, and priority can be claimed in each of these countries or any other member of the International Convention. There are fees for the application, a fee per country and a search fee. The application is filed in one of the three official languages, English, French or German. A search must be requested within approximately 1 year of filing, and the application is published after a period of 18 months from the priority date. After receiving the search report, the applicant must pay a fee for a substantive examination. The application then undergoes an examination in the traditional manner, and if approved, the patent is granted.

The creation of the European patent grant procedure does not affect the existence of the various national grant procedures, and in consequence the inventor is faced with a choice: which route to choose – European or national? The decisive factors will be the value of the protection offered by a European patent, the prospects of obtaining patent protection at all, and the convenience of the procedure.

Value of protection

The European patent is an examined patent, and the examination system has been extended to cover all the contracting states. The European patent has a uniform character, for although the European patent has the effect of a national patent in the contracting states for which it is granted, this effect derives from a uniform legal title, with uniform extent and length of protection, which make for easier administration and improved prospects for the exploitation of the patent.

The administration of affairs relating to the European patent is the responsibility of the European Patent Office, a self-financing organization of over 3500 staff from all the member states, half of whom carry out patent search and examination. The EPO's main work is conducted at Munich, with a searching facility in The Hague and a branch office in Berlin.

Prospects of obtaining patent protection

The EPC does introduce some new features regarding the patentability of inventions (see below), but since the contracting states are aligning their laws with the EPC, the patentability requirements under both European and national law are (or will be) more or less the same. The procedural requirements for obtaining a European patent are the usual ones operating in countries having examination systems, and special care has been taken to protect applicants from the consequences of formal deficiencies or failure to meet time limits.

Convenience of the procedure

The fees to be paid during the European grant procedure have been calculated in such a way that the cost of obtaining a European patent, taking into account the cost of representation and the fact that the proceedings are conducted in one language, will normally be less than the cost of obtaining three corresponding national patents. In addition, an inventor will need to devote substantially less time and effort to a single European procedure than to several national procedures.

The inventor can opt for the language of his preference from among the three official language of the EPO. Translations, which of course do add to the costs, are required by certain contracting states, but these do not have to be provided until the European patent has finally been granted. Until that time, contracting states can only require a translation of the claims.

The European search is comprehensive and very thorough, and the resulting search report provides the applicant with a reliable basis for deciding on whether it is worth continuing with all or only part of the application, so avoiding needless expense. The nature of the search report is considered in more detail below.

The substantive examination stage has been planned in such a way that the procedure is carried out as quickly and cheaply as possible, and in cases in which the applicant files his request for examination before or shortly after the publication of the search report, and does not bring about delays himself, he can expect that the whole grant procedure will be completed about 2 years after filing the European application.

There are inevitably a number of exceptions and special provisions relating to the points outlined above but in general the European patent has become extremely popular, and evidence of this is to be found in the drop in filings in the respective individual countries in favour of the common route. The 1989 annual report of the EPO reported that European and European PCT filings had again increased sharply to approximately 58 000, a figure some 15% up on 1988. By comparison, in 1978, when the first EP applications were filed, the total was 3599.

Patentability

European patents are granted for any inventions which are susceptible of industrial application, which are new, and which involve an inventive step.

The EPC does not define the term 'invention', but gives a non-exhaustive list of items which *cannot* be regarded as inventions, including two areas of special importance, namely-computer programs and methods for the treatment of the human or animal body.

Firstly, computer programs are excluded because of the widely held views that such subject matter is not suitable for patent protection. However, the European patent system acknowledges that there will be difficult borderline cases, and suggests that such matters will have to be settled by the application of case law. The example is cited of a computer-controlled machine tool whose novelty largely depends on its use in a particular combination with a specific computer program.

Secondly, the exclusion of methods for the treatment of the human or animal body by surgery, or therapy and diagnostic methods, does not exclude products, substances and compositions for use in any of these methods, as, for example, medicines or surgical instruments.

On the question of novelty, an invention is considered to be new if it does not form part of the state of the art, which in turn is defined as comprising everything made available to the public by means of a written or oral description, by use, or in any other way, before the date of filing, or the priority date. In addition, prior rights must be taken into consideration, especially as the contents of European patent applications filed prior to the date of filing, or priority date of the invention, and published on or after that date, are considered as comprised in the state of the art insofar as a contracting state named in the later application was also named in the earlier application as published.

An invention will be considered as involving an inventive step if, with regard to the state of the art (but not including prior rights) it is not obvious to a person skilled in the art. The idea of the inventive step requirement is to prevent exclusive rights forming barriers to normal and routine technical development.

European patents search report

The search report for a European patent is provided on a separate sheet as the last page of the specification, and in addition to giving the place of the search, the date on which it was concluded, and the examiner's name, the list also indicates the category or categories of the documents cited. The categories of particular interest to information workers are Category A: technological background, and Category T: underlying theory and principles of the invention. The relevant sections of the documents cited are precisely indicated (page number, line number, and so on) with a reference to the claims involved. Thus the EPO search report goes much further than the United Kingdom practice of simply giving bibliographical details of the publications unearthed.

The majority of applications to the EPO are published as unexamined specifications with a search report attached, and designated A1. Applications for which the search report has been deferred are issued without it as A2 documents. The report subsequently appears, together with the front page of the application, as a document termed A3. An example of a European search report is shown in Figure 2.1.

Commercial databases are increasingly proving their worth as a technical support to search work, and in 1989 it was reported that EPO examiners spent a total of 7089 hours carrying out online searches in 16 939 patent applications, an average time of 25 minutes per application. During the same year the backlog of applications published without a search report was 25 000, compared with 27 000 in 1988.

Formal aspects of a European patent

A European patent application may be filed by any natural or legal person, or anybody equivalent to a legal person, regardless of nationality or place of residence or business. Such a provision enables countries outside Europe, especially the United States and Japan, to obtain protection in countries of their choice, and has proved a very popular route.

When filing a European patent application, the applicant must indicate the contracting states in which he wishes his invention to be protected. Only states for which the EPC has entered into force by the date of filing the European patent application may be designated in the application.

The three official languages of the EPO are English, French and German, but applicants living in a contracting state having a language other than one of those mentioned may file an application in their own official language. This concession however is a short-lived one, for a translation in one of the EPO's official languages must be filed within 3 months after the filing of the European application, or, if the applicant has claimed one or more priorities, the translation must be supplied not later than 13 months after the earliest priority date.

European patent applications must designate the inventor, and if the applicant is not the inventor or is not the sole inventor, the designation of the inventor must be filed in a separate document from the request. Priority may be claimed for a European patent application by a person who, in the 12 months prior to the filing of the application, has filed an application for a patent in any state party to the Paris Convention.

Applicants having their residence or their principal place of business in one of the contracting states may act on their own behalf in proceed-

European Patent
Office

EUROPEAN SEARCH REPORT

Application Number

EP 90 85 0274

DOCUMENTS CONSIDERED TO BE RELEVANT

Category	Citation of document with indication, where appropriate, of relevant passages	Relevant to claim	CLASSIFICATION OF THE APPLICATION (Int. Cl.5)
Y	DE-U-1 986 255 (RÜGGEBERG) * complete document * ---	1	A 01 G 1/08 E 01 C 11/22
Y	US-A-3 491 660 (KWASNEY) * complete document * ---	1	
A	DE-U-1 987 990 (LAMMEL) * claim 1; figure * ---	1	
A	FR-A-2 132 574 (ENTREPRISE BOURDIN & CHAUSSE) * page 4, lines 5-18; figure * ---	1	
A	DE-A-1 658 470 (GUBELA) * claims 1,2 * ---	1	
A	US-A-4 863 307 (JONES) * figures 1,2 * -----	1	
			TECHNICAL FIELDS SEARCHED (Int. Cl.5) A 01 G E 01 C

The present search report has been drawn up for all claims

Place of search	Date of completion of the search	Examiner
BERLIN	07-12-1990	PAETZEL H-J

CATEGORY OF CITED DOCUMENTS

X : particularly relevant if taken alone
Y : particularly relevant if combined with another document of the same category
A : technological background
O : non-written disclosure
P : intermediate document

T : theory or principle underlying the invention
E : earlier patent document, but published on, or after the filing date
D : document cited in the application
L : document cited for other reasons

& : member of the same patent family, corresponding document

Figure 2.1 An example of a European Search Report (with acknowledgement to the EPO)

ings before the EPO. However, applicants not resident in one of the contracting states must engage the services of a representative and act through him before the EPO, in all proceedings other than the actual filing of the European application.

Special procedures apply to the filing of applications for microorganisms, and these are considered in Chapter 12.

Presentation of the invention

For those people using patents as a source of technical information, an understanding of the presentation of the invention is vital, because it enables them to know what to expect and so tailor their searches accordingly.

The European application, as in the case of the British application, must disclose the invention in a manner sufficiently clear and complete for it to be carried out by a person skilled in the art. The application must relate to a single invention only, or to a group of inventions so linked as to form a single general inventive concept. The description, which forms the basis for the claims, must include the following features:

- The title of the invention
- An indication of the technical field to which the invention relates
- An account of the background art, including wherever possible, references to documents reflecting that art
- The disclosure of the invention as claimed, presented in a manner such that the technical problem (even if not expressly stated as such) and its solution can be understood
- A brief description of the figures in any drawings, indicating their numbers
- A detailed account of at least one way of carrying out the invention claimed
- A statement of how the invention is capable of industrial application.

The claims must define the matter for which protection is sought in terms of its technical features, and where appropriate must comprise two distinct parts: a first part designating the subject matter of the invention and the technical features necessary to define it, but which, in combination, are part of the prior art; and a second part characterizing the technical features which, in combination with the first part of the claim, it is desired to protect.

If any drawings form part of the application, they must not contain any textual matter except single words or short phrases, which are exceptionally useful in the better understanding of circuits, block diagrams or flow sheets. The abstract merely serves for use as technical information, and in the case of the European application should not be more than 150 words long. It should be so drafted that it constitutes an efficient instrument for the purposes of searching in the technical field in question, particularly by making it possible to assess whether there is a need to consult the patent application itself. If the application does contain drawings, the applicant should indicate the figure which is most appropriate to accompany the abstract. Unfortunately many abstracts fail to meet these most reasonable of requirements, and a great proportion are not accompanied by a drawing, even though there may be several in the document.

Filing the application

The steps involved in filing a European patent application are similar to those involved in filing a British application (see Chapter 4). The specific requirements are listed in full in the information brochure of the European Patent Office, *How to get a European patent*, the contents of which are revised at regular intervals. The brochure also describes the procedure for the grant of applications, including the various steps up to publication, the publication itself, examination, opposition and appeals.

When all the procedures have been followed, and each stage successfully negotiated, the outcome is the granting of a single European patent equivalent to a 'bundle' of national patents, each of which then has to be individually validated and maintained in the countries still of interest from among those designated at the outset.

Such formalities are very important to applicants seeking patent protection, but fortunately are not of concern to those enquirers simply seeking to consult patents in the European system for the purposes of obtaining technical information.

Information available to the public

Providing the appropriate fees are paid, the files of published European patent applications may be inspected on request, either on the premises of the European Patent Office in Munich or on the premises of the central industrial property office of the contracting state in whose territory the person making the request has his residence or principal place of business.

The EPO keeps a register, known as the Register of European Patents

(REP), giving details of European patent applications and European patents. Extracts from the REP can be obtained on payment of a fee, and it is also possible to have direct access to REP via EURONET.

The EPO also has a number of publishing activities (other than those discussed in Chapter 7) which include an annual report and various information brochures, two of the most important of which are *How to get a European patent – a guide for applicants* and *National law relating to the EPC*. The former publication is intended to give firms, inventors and their representatives an outline of the European procedure for the grant of patents, and, by supplying practical hints, to smooth the way to a European patent, whilst the latter document offers a concise guide to the most important provisions and requirements of the national law of the contracting states applicable to European patent applications and patents, for the use of European patent applicants and proprietors and all others concerned with the European patent system. In particular, the tables outlining the national legal bases serve to emphasize just how much effort has gone into achieving a harmonized European system, paying due regard to the laws and languages of the 14 contracting states. The effort needs to be maintained of course, for with Monaco, Portugal and Finland, among others, expected to accede to the European Patent Convention, the task of harmonization is by no means over.

The Community patent

In addition to the European Patent Convention, another convention, the Convention for the European Patent for the Common Market (Community Patent Convention CPC), has been drawn up, and details were published on 15 December 1975, some 2 years after the conclusion of the EPC. However, political and technical difficulties have so far prevented its coming into force.

A diplomatic conference on the Community patent, held in 1985, succeeded in overcoming some of the problems, and in 1989 all the member states, which by this time had grown from nine to twelve, with a further four waiting for admission to membership, (see Table 2.1) had signed an agreement following the successful conclusion of an intergovernmental conference in Luxembourg.[1]

The Luxembourg Conference found solutions to the outstanding technical problems, namely the scale for the distribution of revenue from fees on Community patents and the arrangements concerning translations. This still left certain political and constitutional difficulties facing two of the member states, Denmark and Ireland, and further work is required on these issues.

The establishment of a Community patent – a unitary patent for the

Community subject to a common system of law, in marked contrast to the 'bundle' of national patents at present available through the European Patent Office – is regarded as an important measure in the completion of the single market, and of course considerable potential benefit to industry in the Community. Until that date arrives, applicants requiring European protection will continue to rely on the European Patent Convention.

Reference

1   Agreement relating to Community patents (1989) *Official Journal of the European Communities* L401, **32**, 30 December, 71 pp.

CHAPTER THREE

Patents in the United States

Whereas the system developed under the European Patent Convention (described in the previous chapter) is of comparatively recent origin, the patent system of the United States of America can trace its origins back to the 18th century, when in 1788 the Constitution, Article 1, Section 8, recorded: 'The Congress shall have power ... to promote the sciences and useful arts by securing for a limited time to authors and inventors the exclusive right to their respective writings and discoveries'. The use of the expression 'to ... inventors' is generally taken as the reason why the United States, alone of all the patenting countries, stipulates that a patent must be applied for by the inventor himself, the 'true inventor' and not by an assignee such as an employer.

The statement in the Constitution was soon followed by the Patent Act of 1790, which provided for a strict examination system. However the concept was quickly proved to be unworkable and in 1793 a change was made to a system of grant without examination. Some 40 years later, in 1836, a systematic examination was reintroduced under the direction of a Commissioner for Patents, and in 1872 the first issue of the *Official Gazette* was published. Today, the files of the United States Patent and Trademark Office represent a store of scientific and technical information so vast and so comprehensive that it ranks in scope with other great American documentation enterprises, such as *Chemical Abstracts*, *Engineering Index* and *Index Medicus*, and constitutes an unrivalled insight into the country's know-how and ingenuity.

On a purely quantitative basis, over 5 000 000 US patents have been issued, and the current size of the output can be judged from the patent numbers allocated over a 5-year period, namely:

Year	Gazette *first & last numbers*	Total
1986	4562596-4633525	70 929
1987	4633526-4716593	83 067
1988	4716594-4794651	78 057
1989	4794652-4890334	95 682
1990	4890335-4980926	90 591

When, on the other hand, it is considered on a qualitative basis, the patent system of the United States has a number of important features which set it apart from systems in use elsewhere in the world. Those of particular importance when using patents primarily as a source of information may be summarized as follows:

● The system allows the inventor an opportunity to develop his ideas before filing an application.

● There is a strict requirement for a prior art statement.

● The system is notable for the absence of early publication

● There is a complex, interactive and sometimes prolonged examination procedure

● The system uses its own domestic classification scheme.

● The published specifications are of a very high standard in terms of lucidity, comprehensiveness and presentation.

United States patent law provides for the granting of patents in three categories:

1. Utility patents, granted to anyone who invents or discloses any new and useful process, machine, manufacture or composition of matter, or any new and useful improvement thereof.

2. Design patents, granted to anyone who has invented a new, original and ornamental design for an article of manufacture.

3. Plant patents, granted to any person who has invented or discovered and asexually reproduced any distinct and new variety of plant, including cultivated sports, mutants, hybrids and newly found seedlings, other than a tuber-propagated plant or a plant found in an uncultivated state.

United States patents are granted for a term of 17 years; in the case of design patents, the term is 14 years.

In looking more closely at the key issues mentioned above, the first point concerns inventions actually made in the United States: the position here is that in contrast with procedures applicable in many other countries, a US patent is granted to the first to invent, and not to the first to file. The practical consequence of this arrangement is that there is far less pressure on a US inventor to get his application on file as quickly as possible, for he knows that provided he has fully documented his invention date (and of course has not suppressed or abandoned his invention in the meantime), he can rely on that date in any conflict with another inventor.

A common way of establishing an invention date, especially by inventors who are working for large corporations or academic institutions, is by means of unpublished evidence such as signed and dated entries in a laboratory notebook. Employers are keen to use this period of consolidation and refinement, and the tendency in the United States is therefore to take longer to define an invention before committing it to paper and filing at the Patent Office, than would be the case for inventions made in other countries. In Europe, for example, ideas are quite frequently filed almost at the moment of conception, and only afterwards is any consideration given to specific embodiments or examples of the invention. Such a practice is one of the reasons why there can be significant differences between what is first revealed in an 'A' specification, and what is eventually published in the 'B' specification.

In the case of inventions filed in the United States but made in other countries, only the US filing date or the date of Convention priority filing can be used. The second point noted above, namely the strict requirement for a prior art search, highlights another important divergence of practice, for although many patenting authorities may require an applicant to state the prior art as cited by other patent offices, there is no obligation to provide anything more than is actually asked for. This is not the case in the United States, where since 1977 it has been incumbent on the applicant to bring to the attention of the Patent and Trademark Office details of all relevant prior art of which he is aware, and indeed the deliberate concealment of any relevant prior art is regarded as a 'fraud on the Patent Office', with appropriately serious consequences both for the patentee and the attorney acting for him.

The requirement for a full disclosure of the prior art, and the longer period in which to refine an application, both enhance the quality of the information contained in a granted patent.

The fact that all relevant prior art has to be brought into the open does not mean that it has to be mentioned in the specification – it may instead form part of the file wrapper, a dossier containing all papers relevant to the prosecution of an application, and eventually available on demand. Where recitals of prior art do occur in a United States specification they are noteworthy for their thoroughness and clarity, and constitute valuable sources of information for anyone seeking to form a picture of the immediate state of the art.

The third point of difference in looking at the United States system is that most developed countries other than the United States now have early publication of unexamined patent applications 18 months from the priority date. In the United States, by contrast, publication of the details of the invention takes place only when the patent is granted, and the delay between the making of an application and the appearance of the issued specification has been a point of frustration for searchers, aware of the existence of a particular application but unable to ascertain its precise contents. The length of the period of delay depends on the length of time it takes to examine the application, and it is the stated aim of the USPTO gradually to reduce the average pendency time for applications to 18 months, so reducing the uncertainty interval to that common elsewhere. Examination is conducted by the military-sounding Patent Examining Corps, comprising Chemical Examining Groups, Electrical Examining Groups, and Mechanical Engineering Examining Groups.

The examination procedure itself is very strict, and consists of a series of official actions and responses with respect to the claims advanced. The intensely interactive nature of the system, sometimes on a face-to-face basis between examiner and inventor, can give rise to a series of appeals and refilings which in difficult cases may go on for a number of years before a patent is finally granted. In some instance this delay may be an advantage, for the 17-year term of protection runs from the date of the grant.

Although the International Patent Classification mark appears on United States specifications, the Patent Office continues to use its own domestic classification, the oldest scheme still in use, having grown from 22 classes in 1830 to a current total of around 350, and one which, some authorities argue, is easy to use.[1] Nevertheless, the scheme needs to be approached with some caution, for, as the Patent Office itself takes pains to emphasize, 'locating patents in a field of technology or science embraced by the US Patent Classification System requires a good measure of judgement applied to the continuous and coordinated use of three tools:

1   The *Index to the Classification*
2   The *Manual of Classification*
3   The *Class and Subclass definitions*'.

The *Index* is an alphabetical list of subject headings referring by indicia numbers to specific patent classes and subclasses. As with other classification schemes the *Index* is most useful as an initial means of entry into the system.

The *Manual of Classification* lists the numbers and descriptive titles of all the classes and subclasses. Titles – more than 100 000 in all – are indicative rather than definitive, and hence necessarily brief.

The *Definitions* comprise statements of the scope embraced by each of the classes and subclasses (except for the plant class and designs), and are supplemented by search notes, the purpose of which is to guide enquirers to related subject matter in other classes and subclasses.

By way of illustration, the example of the classification of the peristaltic pump, employed in the discussion the *United Kingdom Classification Key* (Chapter 4) and the *International Patent Classification* (Chapter 6) can also be deployed to demonstrate the United States form of notation:

USP 4952124 'Medicine injector and method of using same' is classified as: US Cl 417-474 Int Cl^5 F04B 43/12. The number 417 is the general heading used for pumps, and 'pump, peristaltic' can be located from the *Index* as 417 474.

The final point to be noted about United States patents from the information searcher's angle is that the granted specification is a document worth waiting for in terms of clarity and presentation. In addition to the thoroughness of the scene-setting section reviewing the prior art, and the detailed description of the invention itself, the accompanying drawings are presented in a style which is instantly recognizable as embodying particular attention to detail, with careful and consistent use of hatching, directional arrows and the numbering of parts to build up as clear a picture as possible (see Figure 3.1 for an example of a United States specification).

Further consideration of the value and importance of United States patents appears elsewhere in this book, notably in Chapter 7, which deals with announcement and abstracting services; in Chapter 8 which covers patent information networks; in Chapter 9 which examines on line searching methods; and in Chapter 12 which reviews crucial issues in the life sciences.

Reference

1   Dood, K.J. (1979) The US patent classification. *IEEE Transactions on Professional Communications*, **PC22**, 95–100.

United States Patent [19]

Farr

[11]   Patent Number: **4,966,248**

[45]   Date of Patent: **Oct. 30, 1990**

[54]   TRACTION CONTROL SYSTEM

[75]   Inventor: **Glyn P. R. Farr**, Warwick, England

[73]   Assignee: **Lucas Industries public limited company**, Birmingham, England

[21]   Appl. No.:   **231,579**

[22]   Filed: **Aug. 12, 1988**

[30]   **Foreign Application Priority Data**

Aug. 14, 1987 [GB]   United Kingdom 8719299

[51]   Int. Cl.⁵ B60T 8/62
[52]   U.S. Cl. 180/197; 180/244; 303/103; 188/355
[58]   Field of Search .... 180/197, 233, 244, 247, 180/169; 303/114, 93, 111, 110, 113, 119, 116, 61, 62, 63, 100, 99; 188/356, 355, 357, 353, 181; 91/6, 16, 32, 376 R; 60/545, 534

[56]   **References Cited**

U.S. PATENT DOCUMENTS

4,073,359	2/1978	Fujiki et al.	180/169
4,778,225	10/1988	Rudolph et al.	180/197
4,794,538	12/1988	Cao et al.	180/197
4,802,562	2/1989	Kuroyanagi et al.	180/197

Primary Examiner—David M. Mitchell
Assistant Examiner—Richard Camby
Attorney, Agent, or Firm—Scrivener and Clarke

[57]   **ABSTRACT**

A traction control system for the driven wheels of a road vehicle includes a modulation unit which controls fluid flow from a master cylinder actuated via a servo unit to supply fluid under pressure to a spinning driven wheel in order to reduce the degree of spin and increase the torque transmitted to the other driven wheel. The servo unit is actuatable independently and by itself when spin control is required, by way of a solenoid valve which causes a part of the normal output force of the servo to be applied to the master cylinder for the purpose of spin control.

4 Claims, 3 Drawing Sheets

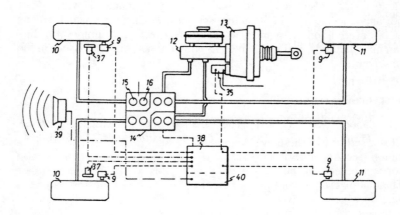

Figure 3.1   Front page of a United States specification (with acknowledgements to the US PTO)

CHAPTER FOUR

Patents in the United Kingdom

What can be patented? The basic requirements relating to patents applied for in the United Kingdom are set out in the Patents Act of 1977 (which came into force on 1 June 1978), and an appreciation of these requirements is important if patents as a source of information are to be exploited successfully.

The 1977 Act says that for an invention to be patentable it must:

● Be new
● Involve an inventive step
● Be capable of industrial application

Closer scrutiny of these three conditions reveals that in the case of anticipation (see Appendix 1, Glossary), it is a requirement for a patent that its concept be new at the date of filing or submission to the Patent Office. The date is critical, and only in a few cases will a disclosure before the date on which the invention was submitted to the Patent Office not be a complete bar or prevention of securing a patent. The disclosure can be by the inventor himself or by a third party. It can also be a disclosure in a patent application which was not published at the time when an inventor submitted his own application, but which nevertheless had an earlier filing date. The following acts are the ones most commonly cited as likely to prevent an inventor obtaining a patent, assuming of course that the disclosure is in fact a description of the invention:

- Presentation of a technical paper at a conference or publication of an article in a magazine
- Sale of the article which constitutes or incorporates the invention
- Description in an earlier relevant patent application, even though that application was not published on the date of the new application
- Discussion of the idea with a third party on a non-confidential basis, as when a salesman tells a potential customer about a new technical development

The second condition relates to an inventive step, a measure designed to ensure that a patent is granted for something which is more than simply novel. The usual way of expressing the concept is to say that the invention must not be obvious, but of course obviousness is hard to determine in the abstract. Consequently the practical test is usually applied, in that the alleged invention must be something beyond that which a normal skilled workman would have tried in the course of his everyday approach to a technology. In other words, the test of an inventive step must be a result which would not easily be reached by one skilled in the art.

Some engineering patent applications, particularly those sought by inventors working on their own, describe an inventive step in the most general terms with no practical embodiment, and supplement it by the sketchiest of drawings, sometimes executed freehand. One result is that the patent literature is enlarged, (some would say cluttered) by applications which have no real chance of proceeding to grant, but which are made in the hope that a benefactor may appear and take over the costs of the proceedings in return for a share of any potential profits.

Applications submitted by companies, on the other hand, are often very detailed, with explanations of a number of practical embodiments, and quite often accompanied by drawings of a quality and clarity suitable for a workshop manual, important points for the information searcher.

The third condition specifies that an invention must be capable of industrial application, a requirement which arose (at least in Great Britain) from the general concept that it was not appropriate that a patent be granted which did not relate to some form of industry, as distinguished from the intellectual arts such as writing, sculpture and so on. In consequence, Section 4 of the 1977 Act states that an invention shall be taken to be capable of industrial application if it can be made or used in any kind of industry, including agriculture.

In one sense, since the concept of industry can be interpreted very widely, the view could be taken that there is hardly an invention which would *not* be capable of some sort of industrial application. However, the situation is clarified by the existence of a number of categories of non-patentable subject matter, each of which needs to be borne in mind before using patents as a source of information. They can be summarized as follows:

● Aesthetic creations such as dramatic and artistic works; schemes, rules or methods for performing a mental act, playing a game or doing business or a presentation of information

● Discoveries (such as the discovery of a law of nature), scientific theories and mathematical methods

● Inventions which are considered offensive, immoral or antisocial

● Methods of treatment of the human body by surgery or therapy, or diagnosis on a human or animal body; this prohibition, as will be noted later, does not apply to pharmaceutical products, and indeed the phrase 'patent medicine' has passed into everyday language.

The above-listed categories constitute the broad span of non-patentable subject matter, and in general the logic behind them is perfectly acceptable, even if difficulties do arise from time to time, as in the case of new board games which might seem suitable candidates for patent protection, but where the preferred action is to seek copyright protection.

Copyright protection is also the approach when dealing with computer programs, although neither the Copyright (Computer Software) Amendment Act 1985 nor the Copyright, Designs and Patents Act 1988 contain a definition of the words 'computer' or 'computer program'. The assumption here must be that the omission was deliberate to ensure that considerable scope would be left to the courts for up-to-date interpretation in a technology which is still undergoing rapid and far-reaching change. The 1988 Act does in fact bring computer programs clearly within the literary fold, for literary works now include computer programs.

Problems regarding inventions of an offensive, immoral or antisocial nature are naturally very subjective in content, and the difficulty of where to draw the line is illustrated by the story of the agreement concluded by the firms Krupp and Vickers in 1902, the subject of which was the Krupp time fuse for artillery shells. Vickers agreed to stamp each of its shells KPz (Krupp Patentzünder) and pay Krupp the sum of one shilling and three pence on each one fired. Should hostilities break out between African or South American clients of the two companies, the arrangement would be relatively harmless. However in the event of war between Great Britain and Germany, Krupp would be seen as profiting from the German casualty lists.

In the event, of course, war did break out, and afterwards in 1921 Krupp filed a claim against Vickers in Sheffield, asking £260 000 for the use of the Krupp fuse during the war. The basis of the claim was that the British had fired over 4 000 000 KPz shells, and a compromise was reached in 1926, when Krupp finally received £40 000[1].

Obtaining a patent

One of the reasons why patents represent such a rich and diverse source of technical information is that the system of protection is open to all, from the individual inventor to the research team backed by the resources of a large corporation.

In describing some of the features of the British system, the first thing to note is that the initial filing fee is very low (currently £15), a fact which encourages the individual inventor in particular, and indeed inventors working for companies, who will be emboldened by a modest fee to press their superiors to protect the inventions which have arisen in the course of their work. However, costs can quickly escalate, and the effort required in terms of time and money should not be underestimated.

Responsibility for the administration of the patent system in Great Britain rests with the Patent Office, the world's oldest industrial property office, which in 1990 became an executive agency of the Department of Trade and Industry, a designation which gives it greater commercial and operating freedom. In addition to its new status, the Patent Office also has a new home in Newport, Gwent.

Although the Patent Office does publish a very helpful layman's guide to the procedure for applying for a patent, it is at pains to point out that obtaining a commercially useful patent requires a high level of expertise, and that anyone who is not thoroughly experienced in patent matters is advised to employ a patent agent.

In the United Kingdom there are about 1250 highly qualified individuals who may legally use the title 'patent agent'. They are qualified by background, experience and examination, and are recognized by the Patent Office to act on behalf of others. A list of registered patent agents may be inspected at the Patent Office. If, as is usually the case, patent agents are in addition members of the Chartered Institute of Patent Agents (CIPA), they may call themselves Chartered Patent Agents.

The qualification rules for patent agents' examinations specify a technical background training to degree level, plus legal training covering all the relevant fields of law. The effort to become a patent agent requires both study and a considerable period (usually 4 or more years) of practice in the office of a qualified agent. There is then a searching examination.

Patent agents belong to a small, highly specialized profession which combines technical and legal skills to form the basis of correct and reliable advice on matters of commercial and financial importance. Nearly all patent agents are male, which may be a reflection of the fact that inventing seems to be a male preserve, for very few ideas are filed by women.

The majority of patent agents work in private practice partnerships, where opportunities arise for them to specialize in certain technologies, and to whom the general public normally turn for advice. In addition, a large number of patent agents work directly for large companies and for government departments.

The 1988 Copyright Designs and Patents Act ended the patent agents' longstanding monopoly by allowing any individual, partnership or body corporate to carry on the business of acting as agents for others for the purpose of applying for and obtaining patents or conducting proceedings before the Comptroller. The outcome is that an unqualified and unregistered person may carry on the business of acting as a patent agent, provided he does not use the title 'patent agent' or 'patent attorney'. The register kept by the Chartered Institute of Patent Agents remains in force, and is regulated by rules which came into effect in 1990, revoking those of 1978.

Whether or not a registered agent is used, the steps involved in applying for a patent can be broken down into two-main parts:

● Preparing the application

● Following the filing and subsequent procedures

Preparing the application involves writing each of the three constituent parts of the specification, namely the description of the invention, the claims which define the invention, and the abstract which summarizes it. In addition, if the invention warrants it, suitable, drawings must be prepared.

The filing procedure is regulated by a series of forms, starting with Patents Form No 1/77 *Request for a grant of a patent*. The specification should contain a full description of the invention, but the claims may be filed later. If they are filed later, they must not add information to that originally filed.

The date on which the completed form 1/77, the description (and any drawings) and the filing fee are received in the Patent Office is the 'date of filing' which will be given to the application. This date affects the patent rights and gives priority over someone else who has a later date, but only in respect of the invention disclosed in the documents filed on that date.

Once the application has a date of filing, the inventor is faced with three choices:

● That after all, it is not worth seeking a patent

● That the application is worth pursuing

● That the best plan is to start again, using the first application to establish a priority date for anything in it which is being put into the new application.

Choice (1) requires no further action and the application will lapse. Choice (2) calls for the filing of Patents Form No 9/77 *Request for preliminary examination and search*, and the payment of the search fee. Choice (3) involves the 'declaration' of the earlier application in the appropriate place on form 1/77.

In the case of a straightforward application, the inventor has 12 months in which to file the claims, the abstract, and form 9/77. If the form is filed, the application is passed to a patent examiner who will search through documents, especially UK patent specifications, which have been published previously, to find any that will need to be considered in determining whether the invention claimed in the specification is either not new or is obvious. The outcome of the examiner's efforts are notified to the inventor in a search report.

The search report enables the inventor to assess realistically the chances of getting over the next hurdle, substantive examination. The application proceeds automatically to the next stage, early publication, unless the inventor specifically requests that the application be withdrawn.

At the early publication stage the contents of the application become available for public inspection, and copies of the specification (the 'A' specification) are put on sale and sent to other patent offices overseas. Early publication normally takes place 18 months after the earliest priority date. An example of an 'A' specification is shown in Figure 4.1

At this point in its life the patent application is a very important document for the information searcher because it offers the earliest opportunity to find out what inventors are working on; it gives an insight into the prior art by virtue of the printed search report; and it carries an abstract which facilitates a rapid assimilation of the idea disclosed.

Within 6 months of early publication, the inventor is faced with another decision and another form. Should he proceed to the substantive examination referred to above? If the answer is yes, Patents Form No 10/77 *Request for substantive examination* must be filed and the examination fee paid. The examiner will then examine the specification to see whether it fulfils the requirements of the Patents Act, with special regard to the following points:

● Does it claim a patentable invention which is new and non-obvious?

● Is the description sufficiently complete and clear for the invention to be made or carried out by someone with a good knowledge of the technical field concerned?

(12) UK Patent Application   (19) **GB**   (11) **2 230 664**(13) **A**

(43) Date of A publication 24.10.1990

(21) Application No 8906448.9

(22) Date of filing 21.03.1989

(71) Applicant
Lucas Industries public limited company

(Incorporated in the United Kingdom)

Great King Street, Birmingham, B19 2XF,
United Kingdom

(72) Inventors
David Anthony Haigh
David Michael Folkard

(74) Agent and/or Address for Service
Marks & Clerk
Alpha Tower, Suffolk Street Queensway,
Birmingham, B1 1TT, United Kingdom

(51) INT CL⁵
H02P 7/00 7/01

(52) UK CL (Edition K)
H2J JDSA JSSS J11P J11VX
U1S S1840

(56) Documents cited
EP 0049649 A1   US 4788490 A   US 4476485 A

(58) Field of search
UK CL (Edition K) H2J JDSA JSAX JSSS JSVF
JSVP, H3P PHAC, H3W WSA WUX WVP WVX
INT CL⁵ H02P
Online databases: WPI

(54) Current drive circuit

(57) A bridge-type current drive circuit is provided for supplying a load such as a torque motor 6. The drive circuit has a first output stage 2 for providing voltage drive to one terminal of the torque motor 6 and a second output stage 3 for providing current drive to the other terminal. The drive circuit is thus capable of continuing to supply current to the torque motor (6) when either motor terminal is short-circuited to ground.

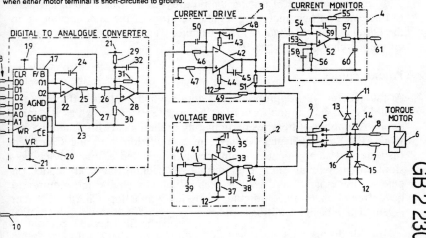

GB 2 230 664 A

At least one drawing originally filed was informal and the print reproduced here is taken from a later filed formal copy.
The claims were filed later than the filing date within the period prescribed by Rule 25(1) of the Patents Rules 1982.
This front page is a reprint to rectify errors introduced in the course of reproduction

Figure 4.1   Front page of a UK 'A' specification (with acknowledgements to the Patent Office)

● Are the claims clear and consistent with what is described?

Eventually, a letter will be despatched informing the inventor of the examiner's conclusions, which will either be that the application complies with the requirements of the act, or that in certain respects it fails to do so. In the latter case a correspondence will ensue until all objections have been overcome and/or appropriate revisions have been made, and the application is considered in order for a patent to be granted. Alternatively, of course, such an exchange of letters may lead to the application's being refused.

For a patent to be granted, the specification must be in order within a period of 4 years and 6 months from the earliest declared priority date. The specification in its granted form may differ from the original application as a result of the changes requested by the examiner, but it will still carry the same seven digit number, this time followed by the letter B (the 'B' specification). The maximum life of the patent, provided renewal fees are paid each year is 20 years from the date of application. No renewal fees are due for the first 4 years of a British patent. The basic features of the British route are repeated, with appropriate local variations, in the paths followed by applicants in other early publication countries.

A number of ways of tracing the progress of a British patent are open to interested parties, including regular scrutiny of the announcements in the *Official Journal (Patents)* (see Chapter 7) and the commissioning of online searches (see Chapter 9).

Patents clinics

At this juncture it is appropriate to mention a helping hand offered to the would-be patentee in the form of an advisory service known as a Patents clinic. A number of libraries participating in the Patents Information Network (PIN) (see Chapter 8) have, in conjunction with the Chartered Institute of Patent Agents, set up locally conducted regular advice sessions for individuals and small businesses seeking basic assistance on patents, trademarks and designs. Patents clinics enable an enquirer to have, free of charge, a 30-minute discussion with a duty Chartered Patent Agent. Three basic conditions apply:

1.   All discussions are in confidence, to avoid damage to any rights subsequently obtained.

2.   The duty patent agent is unable to act for the enquirer but will help find an agent who can.

3.   Because of the limited time available, the advice given cannot be exhaustive and consequently neither the duty patent agent nor the Institute can take responsibility for anything done or not done as a result.

Despite these caveats, the service is well used and very much appreciated – in particular, a valuable benefit is that the counselling session can highlight the need for an inventor to look very carefully at the prior art before incurring any expense. It is at this psychologically crucial moment that the resources of the PIN library hosting the clinic can be brought into play by making available the documents most likely to be of direct help in coming to a decision.

A survey of the usefulness of the Liverpool Patents Clinic[2] covering the start-up months July 1989 – September 1990 yielded replies from 35 users out of a total of 78 mailed. Question 7, 'Before your appointment were you aware of the patent collection at Liverpool City Libraries. or any other patent library and the resources available for exploiting patents?' resulted in 14 people saying yes and 21 saying no; in other words two thirds of the would-be inventors were uninformed as to the scope of the potential help at hand.

The 1949 Act

The procedure for obtaining a patent under the 1977 Patents Act has the virtue of early publication, which enables searchers to see what an inventor seeks to protect just 18 months after the application has been filed.

The procedure adopted under the 1949 Patents Act entailed a much longer interval between application and publication, because no publication took place until the application had been examined and accepted by the Patent Office. Moreover, the specifications published under the 1949 Act did not contain a list of the citations made as a result of an examiner's search, and anyone wishing to know the results of an official search was required to apply to the Patent Office using Patents Form 8, not a particularly convenient route for someone simply looking to establish the state of the prior art.

The 1949 Act provided for a patent term of 16 years, and with the passage of time since the introduction of the provisions of the 1977 Act the number of patents granted under the old legislation and still in force is gradually decreasing, as specifications expire or are not renewed.

The patent specification

The format of a British specification incorporates three essential textual elements, namely an abstract, a description and a set of claims.

The abstract does not constitute part of the patent specification the purpose of defining the invention, but is simply intended to be a statement to the public that will guide them as to the nature of the invention disclosed. Because the abstract is not part of the specification, it can be written in plainer language than the rest of the document. Its purpose is to indicate or inform, and it is often accompanied by one of the drawings from the body of the specification. Its role is similar to that of an abstract of a scientific or technical paper, and properly drafted, it can be of enormous help to someone conducting a patent search. Unfortunately, not all abstracts are helpfully constructed, and quite often consist of a repetition of part of the description or claims, sometimes ending in mid-sentence because of space limitations.

The description is the heart of the document, and will often be accompanied by one or more line drawings. Normally the description will fall into two parts, a discussion of the relationship of the invention to prior knowledge, and an account of the invention by means of examples and references to the drawings if they are included. The requirement to review the closest knowledge published on the invention also varies from country to country; in Great Britain there is no penalty for failing to disclose this type of information to the Patent Office, whereas in the United States the discussion of the prior art is mandatory. From the information searcher's point of view, a thorough and detailed review of the prior art can give valuable leads to other relevant literature, and so considerably enhance the scope of the search. From the inventor's point of view, a discussion of the prior art can be an expensive and time-consuming diversion and he may choose to wait and see what documents the examiner discovers.

Sometimes, however, the inventor may wish to leave the reader in no doubt as to the novelty of his idea, by providing a drawing of the device in question as represented by the current state of the art, and a further drawing of the same device with the inventive modifications applied. In this way a comparison is simple and immediate. The point needs to be made that drawings have to be studied with the text; they carry no explanation themselves apart from a numerical or alphabetical key.

The second part of the description, the technical disclosure, needs to be in sufficient detail to enable the invention to be carried out. A balance has to be struck however, since the specification does not purport to be an instruction sheet and will not carry every piece of information necessary for the exact reproduction of the invention. Instead, it will normally contain sufficient technical information to enable someone skilled in the art, with his normal knowledge, to construct the invention or to reproduce the process. The proviso 'normally' is added here because not all applications do contain sufficient technical information, particularly inventions filed without the benefit of the help of a patent agent.

A concept such as 'a measure of expertise' demands some consideration of just who is meant by someone 'skilled in the art', and the pragmatic view generally taken is a person reasonably skilled in a particular technology without necessarily being the ultimate specialist. In fact, the definition will often depend on the subject matter of a particular patent, and can range from an amateur enthusiast who services his own car (and so will readily understand many automotive inventions) to a highly qualified professional working in a team in a specialized field such as genetic engineering (who may need to consult colleagues on the significance of a specific disclosure).

A third component of the description, no longer an obligation under British law, but which is still strictly applied in the United States, is a requirement to disclose the best mode of carrying out the invention.

The final part of the specification, the claims (or sometimes just one claim), constitutes the definitions of the invention and is precisely worded to give definitions of the actual technology, and not the results of the technology or the aims of the invention. Claims are usually the results of the patent agent's drafting skill, and will customarily start with a first claim comprising a basic statement, followed by specific details of the invention, with subsidiary aspects expanded in subsequent claims. The important question of claims receives further attention elsewhere in this book.

Classification Key

Information workers using material in libraries and other large collections of data will be well versed in the major schemes for the classification of literature as for example the Dewey Decimal System, the Universal Decimal Classification, and the Library of Congress Classification. The main objective of these schemes is to provide a key to a collection which ensures that both staff and users can quickly, effectively and economically find the information from it that they require, prior to the retrieval of the relevant document or documents. As a broad principle, such schemes seek to separate like from unlike, and to proceed in a logical manner from the general to the specific.

Systematic classification schemes are important for shelf arrangement in libraries, but where material is not suitable for arrangement on shelves, as for example reports and abstracts, specialized classification schemes and controlled vocabularies come into play. In the case of information contained in databases, a number of approaches are possible, including thesauri and indexing languages, in addition to natural language systems.

It is something of a culture shock, therefore, to find that the *United Kingdom Classification Key* for patents manages to split the inventive field into just eight main sections, namely:

A   Human necessities

B   Performing operations

C   Chemistry and metallurgy

D   Textiles and paper

E   Civil engineering and building accessories

F   Mechanics, lighting and heating

G   Instrumentation

H   Electricity

These sections are broken down into 40 divisions, which in turn are sub-divided into more than 400 headings. The 40 divisions of the *Classification Key* are also grouped into 25 key units, each containing 1–3 divisions for the purposes of the Patent Office's Abridgment and Abstract services (see Chapter 6). The arrangement of the 25 units runs thus:

Classification Key Unit	Abridgment/Abstract Volume covering division(s)	Subjects Covered
1	A 1-3	Agriculture; animal husbandry; food; tobacco; apparel; footwear; jewellery
2	A 4	Furniture; household articles
3	A 5-6	Medicine; surgery; pesticides; firefighting; entertainment
4	B 1-2	Physical and chemical apparatus and processes
5	B 3	Metalworking
6	B 4-5	Cutting; hand-tools; containing radioactive material; working non-metals; presses
7	B 6	Stationery; printing; writing; decorating
8	B 7	Transport
9	B 8	Conveying; packing; load-handling; hoisting; storing.
10	C 1	Inorganic chemistry; glass; fertilisers; explosives.
11	C 2	Organic chemistry
12	C 3	Macromolecular compounds.
13	C 4-5	Dyes; paints; miscellaneous compositions; fats; oils; waxes; petroleum; gas manufacture.

14	C 6-7	Sugar; skins; microbiology; beverages; metallurgy; electrolysis
15	D 1-2	Textiles; sewing; ropes; paper
16	E 1-2	Civil engineering; building; fastenings; operating doors etc
17	F 1	Prime movers; pumps.
18	F 2	Machine elements
19	F 3-4	Armaments; projectiles; heating; cooling; drying; lighting
20	G 1	Measuring; testing
21	G 2-3	Optics; photography; controlling; timing
22	G 4-6	Calculating; counting; checking; signalling; data handling; advertising; education; music; recording; nucleonics
23	H 1	Electric circuit elements; magnets
24	H 2	Electric power
25	H 3-5	Electronic circuits; radio receivers; telecommunications; miscellaneous electric techniques

The *Classification Key* was originally designed to assist Patent Office examiners in their novelty searches, not to help the public to find a patent for an object with a definite use. The schedules also reflect the points made earlier, that inventions must be capable of industrial application, and that theories and concepts fall outside the scope of the system.

The *Classification Key* is continually being revised, and the descriptive terms in the edition that is operative in a given period (e.g. a year) and that are applied to specifications published and/or classified in that period may not be available for use in specifications classified in earlier or later periods. In addition, for specifications published prior to the introduction of the Patents Act 1977, the issue of the *Key* that appears in an Abridgment volume may be accurate only for the span of publications covered by that volume. Thus it is vital to keep a note of *Key* changes, and for this purpose the editions are identified by capital letters, commencing with A for editions from of 1 January 1979 onwards. An indication of the edition used is given on the front page of the specification itself, under item (58) Field of search.

Given the complexity of the *Classification Key* schedules, with their frequent resort to explanatory notes, it is clear that to use the system effectively requires considerable skill, practice and patience. The 400 or so headings mentioned above are broken down into specific indexing terms identified by codes. For example, division F 1 covers prime movers and pumps, and is broken down into:

F 1   B   Internal combustion engines etc
       C   Non-positive displacement pumps etc
       D   Hydraulic and pneumatic actuators etc
       E   Injectors and ejectors
       F   Rotary positive displacement devices
       G   Gas turbine plant
       H   Spray carburettors
       J   Jet propulsion plants
       K   Starting, stopping, reversing engines etc
       M   Steam engines etc
       N   Miscellaneous compressors, vacuum pumps etc
       P   Fluid pressure apparatus
       Q   Power plant
       R   Raising and discharging liquids etc
       S   Miscellaneous prime movers
       T   Turbines
       U   Peristaltic devices
       V   Bladed rotors and stators
       W   Fluid pressure reciprocating machines
       X   Miscellaneous fluid appliances

A closer look at F 1U reveals a definition which states that 'the subject matter with which this heading is concerned is peristaltic devices such as pumps, motors or meters, i.e. devices including a flexible tube or equivalent member, the cross-section of which is varied in a progressive or sequential manner along the tube length, the contents either being acted upon by the tube, e.g.being transported along the tube as in a pump or acting on the tube e.g. to generate mechanical energy as in a motor or meter'.

The accompanying indexing schedule lists a variety of specific features:

U1   kinds or types which do not use a smooth surface
U2   cooling and heating
U3   facilitating replacement of components
U4   governing and regulating
U5   hand-operated
U6   plural devices
U7   special materials
U8   motor or meter

Thus GB 2208896 A, peristaltic pump cartridge, is classified as: F 1U UA U3 U6.

The *Classification Key* draws attention to the fact that 'the subject matter corresponds approximately with... subclasses... in the International Patent Classification', and the degree of correspondence is discussed in Chapter 6.

The first step in a subject search is a clarification of the subject terms to be searched for, which must be expressed as precisely as possible. The next stage is to consult the catchword index to the *Classification Key*, which is in essence an access tool consisting of an alphabetical list of 'catchwords' identifying subjects (articles or operations) in which the invention is likely to occur. A catchword may be followed directly by the code of the heading under which the subject represented by the catchword may be found. It is more likely, however, that the code will be followed by detailed references which place the term in its proper context.

Once the correct indexing code has been determined, confirmation must be sought by referring to the appropriate place in the *Classification Key* itself, where the scope notes will enlarge on what the term embraces and what it excludes, with guidance on where in the *Key* the exclusions are to be found. The specific aspects of the subject can then be sought by examining the detailed tables, until an extended code is found which matches the concept in question.

Care must be taken that codes are not overlooked as other relevant aspects of a subject may appear at different positions in the tables, each with their own codes.

A feature of the tables is the indication of 'term frequency', a statement which tells the user that at the last check a specific number of specifications had been assigned the term in question. Thus it is possible to proceed from an idea expressed in everyday language to a code which pinpoints the relevant patents and indicates how many there are likely to be. In an ordinary collection of literature the next step would be to go direct to the shelves or files, and there consult the documents identified. However, with patents there are still more features to be considered before the search can be regarded as complete.

As noted earlier, the *Classification Key* was designed first and foremost to assist Patent Office examiners. The classifying terms are abstract and function-oriented wherever possible, with the result that the applications of the invention are not obvious from the terms applied. One of the worst offenders in this respect was recognized in 'coated products', and an example of the practical difficulties encountered has been described by Arnott[3], who refers to a carbon coating invented to coat an artificial heart valve, and so make it more acceptable to the body. The invention was classified under 'coated products' only, and so became lost to any searcher looking for advances in artificial organs.

In 1983, following representations from the community of industrial patent searchers, the Universal Indexing Schedules (UIS) were introduced with effect from Edition E of the *Classification*, in an attempt to make retrieval easier for the public. The Schedules are for 'Use Application Utility and Property', and where appropriate a code is allocated to a patent specification in addition to the usual codes from the *Classification Key*. The Schedules are arranged in three parts: Part One contains the heading codes for the rest of the *Classification*; Part Two gives uses and applications of inventions in the following broad sequences, encompassing some 1300 headings:

● Recovering and reclaiming materials
● Naturally occurring and living entities
● Manufactured materials technology
● Energy technology
● Information and control technology
● Special environments

Each of these sequences devolves into lists of indexing terms, with the prefix S. Part Three, which consists of utilities and properties, is not truly universal by virtue of the fact that it can only be applied to about 29% of the 400 indexing terms noted above, and consists of the following sequences:

● Life processes
● Chemical activity
● Relations with other materials
● Surface properties
● Flow, mechanical, weight, thermal, sound, electrical, optical and radiation properties

Inevitably there are overlaps between Parts Two and Three, and a further problem is knowing when to stop when seeking to allocate the indexing terms. In particular, with specifications which cite multiple uses of an invention, classifiers clearly have to use a measure of discretion and concentrate on the significant items.

The UIS is supplemented by a catchword index of its own, primarily intended to be used as an aid to finding a particular term in UIS, rather than as a substitute to the use of the UIS themselves. An example is contained in the concept of 'preventing':

Compositions for preventing
    corrosion   S 1349
    freezing   S 1406
    misting   S 1371

oxidation	S 1349
slipping	S 1363
fire and explosions	S 1178–1181
theft	S 2188

The Patent Office has issued three pamphlets which provide more help on matters of classification, namely:

1. 'Structure of the Classification Key', listing the headings grouped under each of the 40 divisions
2. 'Notes on the use of the Classification Key'
3. 'Heading UIS Universal Indexing Schedules for Use Application, Utility and Property'

One of the advantages of a tightly controlled classification system with relatively short alphanumeric codes is that it permits the compilation of subject matter file-lists such lists are available in three series:

Series A File-lists cover specifications published from the year 1911 up to an easily remembered serial number, 1 000 000 (July 1965). The lists are organized according to the edition of the *Classification Key* in force in 1965, and consequently the codes specified must be drawn from the edition for the Series 960 001 to 1 000 000 (the 960 *Key*). *Series C and D File-lists* are produced by computer on request, with the range of specification numbers covered depending on the heading concerned. In all the headings the range includes specification numbers from 1 000 000 to the present, whilst for certain headings the range extends backwards from 1 000 000, mostly to the year 1925.

Series C File-lists can be ordered for any single code mark, and will include applications published by the European Patent Office and under the Patent Cooperation Treaty. *Series D File-lists* can be ordered for combination searches of two or more code marks, using the usual algebraic expressions AND/OR and NOT, a facility touched upon in Chapter 8, which covers online searching.

Although in theory it is possible to search using a combination of up to 100 code marks, in practice the usual constraints associated with complicated searches will apply, and the recall/relevance ratio will depend on how widely or how narrowly the question is formulated. In other words, specificity, the degree to which it is possible to designate exact subjects, will increase relevance at the cost of recall, whereas exhaustivity, the extent to which the subject of a patent is analyzed by the examiner when creating a file, will increase recall and decrease relevance.

Once a searcher has acquired a file-list, the next step is to find out the scope of each specification listed. This can be done by referring to the specifications themselves, available at selected libraries or through special supply services (see Chapter 8) or by consulting abstracts and abridgments published by the Patent Office, or abstracts issued by commercial and other concerns (see Chapter 7).

United Kingdom publications

Publications issued by the British Patent Office (other than the *Official Journal (Patents)* and the pamphlets service for *Abstracts*, both discussed in Chapter 6) which are of special use to information searchers and users include a name index, an annual report, and booklets on how to obtain a patent and how to use patents as a source of information.

The name index is an annual volume published as *Names of Applicants*, and contains entries for applications made in a calendar year. A brief indication is provided of the subject matter of each application and individual inventors are cross-referenced, if appropriate, to the companies for which they work. Later volumes contain classification numbers. A document which usually gets noticed in the general press is the *Annual Report of the Comptroller General of Patents, Designs and Trade Marks*,[4] and it is a particularly useful compilation from an information searcher's point of view, in that it highlights trends of inventions in published specifications. The 1991 report tabled the numbers of specifications by main subject matter, and the top five subject areas in 1990 were as follows (see also Table 4.1):

			App'ns	Grants	Total
1	F2	Machine elements	966	803	1769
2	F4	Measuring and testing	789	639	1428
3	B8	Conveyancing, packaging etc	763	556	1319
4	H1	Electric circuit elements	582	555	1137
5	E1	Civil engineering; building	733	382	1115

The booklet '*Patents – a source of technical information*' is aimed at industry, research and development units, universities, polytechnic, inventors, engineers and scientist, and seeks to explain 'the facilities made available by the UK Patent Office for enabling the information in published patent documents to be searched and for enabling a watch to be kept on applications made by particular companies or individuals, e.g. competitors'. The booklet is especially useful in explaining in a succinct manner the workings of the *Classification Key*.

Finally, as with many other patent offices, the British Patent Office publishes from time to time a layman's guide to the procedure for applying for a patent under the 1977 Act, which takes the form of a pamphlet '*How to prepare a UK patent application*'. It is suggested that by using the guide it is possible, without professional assistance, to prepare and file a patent application and to follow it through to grant of a patent. The pamphlet does not deal with the question of whether an invention is likely to be patentable, although very general information on such matters is given in another publication, '*Introducing patents*'.

Checklist of legislation

The following Acts of Parliament (Statutes) relating to intellectual property are still in force, although most of the sections of the first two items have been repealed.

Statute of Monopolies 1623 (c.3)

Patents and Designs Act 1907 (c.29)

Chartered Associations (Protection of Names and Uniforms)
Act 1926 (c.26)

Trade Marks Act 1938 (c.22)

Patents Act 1949 (c.87)

Registered Designs Act 1949 (c.88)

Defence Contracts Act 1958 (c.38)

Patents Act 1977 (c.37)

Trade Marks (Amendment) Act 1984 (c.19)

Patents Designs and Marks Act 1986 (c.36)

Copyright Designs and Patents Act 1988 (c.48)

To the above must be added details of subordinate legislation in the form of Statutory Instruments, made by ministers under the authority of spe-

Table 4.1 UK Patent Office requests for grant

Year	Without claim to priority	With claim to priority	Total
1983	18 363	16 328	34 961
1984	17 664	15 164	32 828
1985	18 362	13 603	31 965
1986	18 978	12 125	31 103
1987	19 202	11 162	30 364
1988	20 134	10 337	30 471
1989	19 425	9 944	29 369
1990	19 277	8 961	28 238

cific Acts and dealing with matters of a detailed, and sometimes temporary, nature. The most important of these are the Patents Rules (SI 1990/2384), which replace the Patents Rules 1982 and subsequent amendments; and the Register of Patent Agents Rules (SI 1990/1457) which revokes the 1978 Rules.

In addition, it should be noted that the Copyright Designs and Patents Act 1988 was the repealing enactment for the following statutes:

Copyright Act 1956 (c. 74)

Patents and Designs (Renewals Extensions and Fees) Act 1961 (c. 75)

Design Copyright Act 1968 (c. 68)

Copyright (Amendment) Act 1971 (c. 4)

Copyright Act 1956 (Amendment) Act 1982 (c. 35)

Copyright (Amendment) Act 1983 (c. 42)

Copyright (Computer Software) Amendment Act 1985 (c. 41)

References

1. Manchester, W. (1969) *The arms of Krupp*. London: Michael Joseph, pp. 255, 381
2. Cole, R.D. (1991) Liverpool Patents Clinic. *World Patent Information* **13**, (1), 17-20
3. Arnott, R. (1979) British patent classification. *Journal of the Chartered Institute of Patent Agents*, Part 1, April, 287-291; Part 2, June, 381–386
4. *107th annual report of the Comptroller-General of Patents, Designs and Trade Marks (1990)*. London: Her Majesty's Stationery Office (HC 399)

CHAPTER FIVE

Patents in some major industrialized countries

Industrialized market economies

Although over 120 countries are party to the convention establishing the World Intellectual Property Organization, only a handful are considered sufficiently important for the owners of inventions to seek patent protection in them as a matter of routine. Part of the reason for this discrimination is the avoidance of multiplying costs, and partly the unattractive commercial advantages available in many of the countries.

Of the countries which are commonly selected (typically those which also belong to the Organization for Economic Cooperation and Development (OECD), the instrument for international cooperation among industrialized nations on economic and social policies), the space available in this book precludes a consideration of all but a significant few. Thus attention is confined to Germany, Japan, and (representing the southern hemisphere) Australia. The patent systems of each country will be considered briefly in the light of the special interests and requirements of the information searcher, whilst the main features of the official publications will be looked at in Chapter 7.

The level of patenting activity in each of the countries mentioned is summarized in Table 5.1. The figures are based on the WIPO compilation *Industrial Property Statistics*,[1] and relate to the year 1989. For the purposes of comparison, attention is restricted to applications made by residents of the countries concerned, using the national route only (i.e. ignoring applications which specify the Patent Cooperation Treaty or the European Patent Convention, and applications made by non-residents).

Table 5.1 Level of patenting activity

Country	Population	Applications
Australia	16.6m	6 050
Germany (FR)	61.1m	31 171
Japan	121.8m	317 353

Table 5.1 shows that the total number of applications filed in Japan is far ahead of the applications received by the other patenting authorities, and indeed the only country which comes anywhere near the Japanese total is the Soviet Union, which for the same year recorded a figure of 145 266 inventors' certificates. An inventor's certificate is a form of recognition granted for a period of 15 years to an inventor, which gives him no actual monopoly rights, since the invention is freely available for use by the State. Instead of the traditional rights, the inventor receives benefits such as cash awards or payments in kind, and the inventor's certificate system has been compared to the employee suggestion and incentive schemes which operate in many large companies in Europe and elsewhere.

Germany

In Germany the patent system has had a considerable influence upon the development of the European patent system, and from the technology-watcher's viewpoint two traditions of great importance have been the practice of early publication, and the stylized manner of stating the claims.

Before the unification of the country in 1871 there were nearly 30 different patent authorities in the various independent German states. The first patent unifying law was passed in 1877, but with the formal establishment in October 1949 of the German Democratic Republic this unity was broken, with an arrangement which led to the parallel publication of DE (Federal) and DD (Democratic) patent specifications.

On 3 October 1990 Germany once again became a single country, and the European Commission estimated that 80% of the single market legislation could apply immediately to the former German Democratic Republic, including that on intellectual property. The immediate practical effect of the reunification was that patent applications filed from 3 October 1990 onwards, for the whole of the enlarged country, would be published as Offenlegungsschriften with the country code DE. East German applications filed prior to 3 October would continue to be treated as exclusive patents according to the laws of the German Democratic Republic, and still designated by the country code DD.

The present remarks, however, are confined to the system in the Federal Republic, where two types of patent can be obtained, the patent proper and the utility model (Gebrauchsmuster), identified by the initials GM.

The German Patent Office makes a point of differentiating between the patent and the utility model by stressing that the former costs more to obtain, is only granted after examination, and has a maximum term of 20 years. The utility model on the other hand is registered without examination (although a prior art search can be requested to assist in the evaluation of registrability), its fees are nominal, and the term of protection is 10 years.

Utility models are a form of patent protection considered and rejected in Great Britain in the White Paper *Intellectual Property and Innovation* (1986).[2] In Germany, the subject matter eligible for protection in this manner includes working tools and implements, and articles of everyday use, provided they show a new configuration, arrangement, device or circuit, involve inventiveness, and are susceptible to industrial application.

Specifications are now classified by the International Patent Classification, but for nearly 100 years the influential Deutsche Patentklassifikation (DPK) was used both by Germany and many other European states, until the seventh edition was superseded in 1975.

The procedure for obtaining a German patent is in two stages, namely a prior-art search followed by a substantive examination, in which the examiner applies the cited prior art to determine whether or not the invention is patentable. The two stages can be carried out quite separately, so that the applicant may request a search on opposition and then wait several years before requesting substantive examination.

Early publication of applications has always been an important source of up-to-date technical information, and often constitutes the closest prior art against subsequent applications. In Germany up to 1980, patents were published three times, namely:

1. Offenlegungsschriften (unexamined applications) DOS

2. Auslegeschriften (examined applications) DAS

3. Patentschriften (granted patents) DPS

In 1981, the procedure was simplified by the omission of the DAS stage, although provision for belated opposition after the publication of the DPS was retained.

DOS were always important to information searchers in the days when other countries such as Great Britain did not have a system of early publication. Filing first in Great Britain and then in Germany often meant that the details of the invention were available in the DOS before the British patent was published. Nowadays, when early publication is the norm in Europe and elsewhere, the availability of Offenlegungsschriften is still very important because German industry is such a prolific source of applications for patents.

The claims of a German patent are normally drafted to distinguish what is old from what is new, with the first part of the first claim containing a 'precharacterizing clause' which recites what is already known. Then comes the expression 'characterized in that' (dadurch gekennzeichnet), which introduces the characterizing clause stating what is the novel feature of the invention. This style of claim is favoured but not insisted upon by the European Patent Office.

As ever, the abstract is of major importance for the information searcher; in Germany the abstract normally appears with the DOS document, but if for some reason it is not published then, the abstract appears as part of the DPS document.

Japan

The Japanese patent system is difficult enough to use simply because of the language barrier; it is also characterized by a system of dates, which is totally different from practice in the rest of the world. From the information searcher's point of view there is a need to place a heavy reliance on abstracts (details of which are given in Chapter 6) rather than on the original Japanese texts. The more important characteristics to note about patents in Japan are the practice of early publication, the use of main and utility patents, and the very large annual output of unexamined applications.

The term of right of protection is 15 years (10 years for utility models) from the date of the publication of the examined application, provided that it does not exceed 20 years (15 years for the utility model) from the filing date. New patent law which came into effect in January 1988 has altered the concept of unity of invention, and from that date onwards every claim filed in an application is considered as a single invention. Previously only an independent claim (although associated with multiple dependent claims) in an application was considered as a single invention. There is now a separate fee for each claim in an application.

An unexamined application is laid open to public inspection after 18 months, in the form of a document called a Kokai Tokkyo Koho, and a Kokai number is allocated. The date is expressed in a special way; thus in application no. 63–22618, the numerals 63 indicate the 63rd year of

Showa (the period of the Emperor Hirohito's reign), that is AD 1988, calculated from the year of his accession, which was 1925. Examination of applications is by request only, which must be made within 7 years of the filing date, or in the case of a utility model, within 4 years. The outcome is the publication of the application in its examined form, known as a Tokkyo Koho, to which is allocated a Kokoku Koho number. The examined patent is eventually published a third time as a registered patent complete with a patent serial number. As noted in Chapter 8, it is important to keep these distinctions in mind when searching databases for Japanese items.

Using Japanese patents as a source of information is no easy task, because apart from the considerations noted above, there is also the problem of the sheer quantity of the documentary output. As indicated in Table 5.1, the number of national applications in 1989 was 317 353, representing a flood of ideas emerging at the rate of 870 for every single day of the year, making the Japanese by far the most prolific applicants in the world.

Australia

The Patent Cooperation Treaty provides for an international search to be carried out by any of a small number of the major patent offices throughout the world, and the Patent Office of Australia is one of those so designated – the only one in the southern hemisphere, in fact.

Australia is also one of the major offices which can be used when an applicant under the PCT procedure chooses to ask for an international preliminary examination report giving a preliminary and non-binding opinion on the patentability of the claimed invention.

The Australian patent system has numerous features which are based on British practice before the reforms of 1977, and inventors have the choice of applying for a standard patent having a duration of 16 years from the date of lodging the complete specification, which is subject to examination by direction or voluntary request, or for a petty patent having a duration of 1 year from the date of grant, with a possible extension to a total of 6 years.

In preparing his specification, the inventor is not required to write a summary, and in citing the prior art, a 'book, specification or other work shall not be referred to unless it is available to the public in Australia and is fully identified in the specification'.

The Australian Patent Office issues a series of pamphlets covering general matters, including *Patents in Australia, Basic facts about patents for inventions, How to prepare an Australian patent application* and *Patents – a guide for inventors*, with more detailed matters being discussed in a further series covering *Provisional specifications for patents, Examination of a patent application*, and *Patents of addition and further applications.*

Special characteristics

Each of the countries chosen as representatives of the world's national patent systems has special characteristics of particular interest to the information searcher.

The German system exerts an influence which has been carried over into the European system; the Japanese system is remarkable for the large number of applications it receives each year; and the Australian system is an example of those which retain certain features based on their British origins.

References

1. International Bureau (1990) *Industrial property statistics*. Geneva: World Intellectual Property Organization (Publication A – supplement to *Industrial Property*, 11, 1990)
2. *Intellectual property and innovation* (1986) London: Her Majesty's Stationery Office (Cmnd 9712)

CHAPTER SIX

International aspects

The 'world patent'

At this juncture it is appropriate to mention a point of principle which all national patent offices seek to emphasize in their introductory pamphlets for applicants – namely that there is no such thing as a 'world patent'. The advice usually given is that an inventor must lodge an application in each country. in which protection is required, and that an alternative approach is to file an International Application under the Patent Cooperation Treaty. Such an application provides the basis of separate national applications in a wide range of countries, as will be seen below.

The need to stress the fact that patents are a territorial form of protection is not just a case of stating the formal position. There is widespread evidence, judging from the frequent reports in the popular press, that inventors really do think they can obtain worldwide patents, or acquire, international protection for their ideas, at a stroke.

The Patent Cooperation Treaty

In addition to the opportunities open to the inventor to protect his idea by filing an application at the national office of his country of residence, or at the European Patent Office in Munich, there is the route provided by the Patent Cooperation Treaty (PCT), which is intended to minimize the costs of the procedures resulting from international filings.

The treaty, which was concluded on 19 June 1970 has, some 20 years later, 45 contracting states (compared with 100 states which are party to the Paris Convention), and provides for the filing of an 'international' patent application by residents or nationals of contracting states. The application has to be filed with the national patent office of the contracting state, or, if the applicant is a national or resident of a contracting state which is party to the European Patent Convention (EPC), the international application may also be filed with the European Patent Office. If the applicant is a national or resident of a contracting state which is a member of the African Intellectual Property Organization (OAPI), or lives in Barbados or Sri Lanka, then the international application has to be filed with WIPO in Geneva.

Out of the 45 contracting states (the most recent of which are Spain, 1989, and Canada, Greece and Poland 1990) the applicant designates those in which he wishes his international application to have effect. The effect of any international patent application in each designated state is the same as if a national patent application had been filed with the appropriate national office.

The international application is then subjected to what is termed an 'international search', carried out by one of the major patent offices, namely those in Australia, Austria, Japan, the Soviet Union, Sweden and the United States, or by the European Patent Office. The outcome is an International Search Report listing documents which might affect the patentability of the invention, and on the basis of the report's findings the applicant is in a position to decide whether to proceed, perhaps with some appropriate amendments, or whether to withdraw.

The International Search Report (an example of which is shown in Fig. 6.1) places each relevant document identified into one of a considerable number of categories. Category 'A' is used to identify a 'document defining the general state of the art which is not considered to be of particular relevance', whilst Category 'X' is applied to a 'document of particular relevance; the claimed invention cannot be considered novel or cannot be considered to involve an inventive step', a judgement which must make unwelcome reading for the applicant. Almost as discouraging is Category 'Y', which refers to a 'document of particular relevance; the claimed invention cannot be considered to involve an inventive step when the document is combined with one or more other such documents, such combination being obvious to a person skilled in the art'.

The International Search Report thus has the virtue of concentrating an applicant's mind; if the evidence presented is overwhelmingly against the case for the claimed invention, the application can simply be abandoned; if the evidence is open to interpretation, the matter can be referred back to the inventor, who may be able to work out an alternative approach; or if the evidence is favourable, the application can proceed.

One of the features of the PCT is that it provides that a search shall be carried out through what it terms 'minimum documentation', which consists of all patents published since 1920 in important countries, and a selection of key journals which publish material likely to be useful to in-

INTERNATIONAL SEARCH REPORT

International Application No PCT/HU90/00062

I. CLASSIFICATION OF SUBJECT MATTER (If several classification symbols apply, indicate all)⁶

According to International Patent Classification (IPC) or to both National Classification and IPC

Int.Cl.5   B60C 27/04

II. FIELDS SEARCHED

Minimum Documentation Searched

Classification System	Classification Symbols
Int.Cl.5	B60C 27/00, 27/02, 27/04, 27/06, 27/16, 27/20

Documentation Searched other than Minimum Documentation
to the Extent that such Documents are included in the Fields Searched

III. DOCUMENTS CONSIDERED TO BE RELEVANT⁹

Category*	Citation of Document¹¹ with indication, where appropriate, of the relevant passages¹²	Relevant to Claim No.¹³
A	EP,A, 0 147 272 (R. GOURHANT) 3 July 1985 (03.07.85), see figures 1-9	(1,3)
A	US,A, 4 209 049 (J. REGENSBURGER) 24 June 1980 (24.06.80), see figures 1-4	(1)
A	DE,B2, 2 400 831 (ELKEM-SPIGERVERKET A/S) 28 July 1977 (28.07.77) see figures 1-3	(1)
A	DE,A1, 3 423 959 (ELKEM A/S) 24 January 1985 (24.01.85), see figures 1-5	(1)
A	US,A, 3 053 302 (J. H. BOPST III) 11 September 1962 (11.09.62) see figures 1,2	(1,2)
A	FR,A, 2 160 340 (J. MONANGE) 29 June 1973 (29.06.73), see figures 4,6	(2)
A	US,A, 2 912 036 (L. C. MINUTILLA) 10 November 1959 (10.11.59), see figures 3,4	(3)

* Special categories of cited documents: ¹⁰
"A" document defining the general state of the art which is not considered to be of particular relevance
"E" earlier document but published on or after the international filing date
"L" document which may throw doubts on priority claim(s) or which is cited to establish the publication date of another citation or other special reason (as specified)
"O" document referring to an oral disclosure, use, exhibition or other means
"P" document published prior to the international filing date but later than the priority date claimed

"T" later document published after the international filing date or priority date and not in conflict with the application but cited to understand the principle or theory underlying the invention
"X" document of particular relevance: the claimed invention cannot be considered novel or cannot be considered to involve an inventive step
"Y" document of particular relevance: the claimed invention cannot be considered to involve an inventive step when the document is combined with one or more other such documents, such combination being obvious to a person skilled in the art
"&" document member of the same patent family

IV. CERTIFICATION

Date of the Actual Completion of the International Search	Date of Mailing of this International Search Report
9 November 1990 (09.11.90)	14 November 1990 (14.11.90)

International Searching Authority	Signature of Authorized Officer
Austrian Patent Office	

Form PCT/ISA/210 (second sheet) (January 1985)

Figure 6.1   Example of an International Search Report (with acknowledgements to WIPO)

ventors. The selection takes the form of a list agreed in 1978 and subject to regular updates. The number of titles it contains is now approaching 200[1], a very modest total considering the thousands of scientific and technical periodicals issued each year. If, in the light of the evidence provided by the International Search Report, the applicant does decide to continue, the application, together with the search report, is processed and published by WIPO, and the details are communicated to each of the designated patent offices,

20 months after filing the international application, or, where the application involves the priority of an earlier application, 20 months after the filing of the earlier application, and not before, the applicant is required to provide each designated office with a translation of the application into its official language, with the payment of the appropriate fees. This 20-month period can be extended by a further 10 months if the applicant chooses to ask for an 'international preliminary examination report'. Such a report is prepared by one of the major patent offices (i.e. those listed above plus the United Kingdom) and constitutes a preliminary and non-binding opinion on the patentability of the invention.

The procedure under the PCT is claimed to benefit the applicant, the patent offices and the public as follows:

1.   The applicant has 8 or 18 months more than he has in a procedure outside the PCT, to reflect on the desirability of seeking protection in foreign countries, for appointing local patent agents, for preparing the required translations and paying the national fees.

      Moreover, on the basis of the international search, and especially on the basis of the international preliminary examination report, he can evaluate with reasonable probability the chances of the application's succeeding.

2.   The search and examination work of the patent offices is considerably reduced as a result of the search report, and where applicable, the preliminary examination report.

3.   Since each international application is published with a search report, any member of the public can form his own conclusion on the patentability of the invention in question.

On the down side it has to be noted that there is little saving once national proceedings have commenced, and, because of the relative complexity of the procedure, there is a greater possibility of error and possible loss. WIPO publishes a *PCT Applicant's Guide* as a loose leaf compilation in two volumes: Volume 1 contains general information on the PCT intended for those interested in filing international patent applications;

Volume 2 explains the procedures before designated or elected patent offices. Together the two volumes run to over 600 pages.

General experience seems to indicate that the PCT system is valuable for applications which need to be filed at very short notice in the relevant countries, and it is frequently used by smaller applicants of limited financial means, who must look for every stratagem which helps to postpone expense. However, the popularity of the system is clearly growing (see Figure 6.2) and the increase in filings, which averaged 27.7% per year in the three years 1988–1990, can be attributed mainly to the increasing awareness of inventors, industry and patent attorneys of the advantages offered by the PCT.

In comparison with the European patent system, it will be seen that the PCT route has the more limited objective of conducting the initial examination and search at the international level, before passing the case to the individual patent offices involved for full examination and grant. Since, however, it is the technical information content of the application which

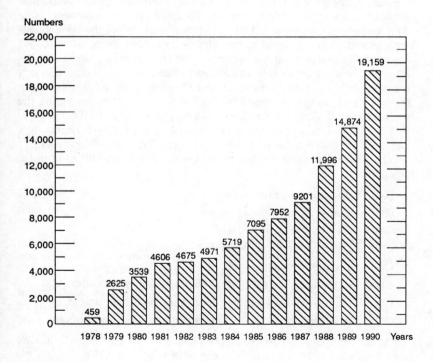

Figure 6.2   The increase in filings by the PCT route since the system began in 1978. (With acknowledgements to WIPO)

is of prime interest to the searcher, the ultimate form of publication through the national office is of secondary concern.

Bibliographic data on patent documents

Many countries now include in their patent documents code numbers (internationally agreed numbers for the identification of bibliographic data – INID codes), usually on the first page, which serve to identify items of bibliographic data including priority information, names, application number and date. A major advantage of the codes is that they facilitate the recognition of items of data by readers unfamiliar with the language of the document.

These codes have been prepared by ICIREPAT (International Cooperation in Information Retrieval Between Examining Patent Offices) with the recommendation that they should be associated with the corresponding data elements, insofar as these elements normally appear on the first page of a document. Preferably the codes should be indicated using Arabic numerals within small circles immediately before the corresponding element. It is important to note that if data elements to which codes are normally assigned do not appear on the first page of a document because they are not applicable, or for some other reason, it is not necessary for the publishing office concerned to call attention to the non-existence of such elements (for example by leaving a space, or by providing the relevant code followed by a dash). A good example is INID code (55) Keywords, which appears on patents issued by the German Democratic Republic but not on those issued by the Federal Republic of Germany.

The list of data elements has been organized into the following broad categories:

(10)   Document identification

(20)   Domestic filing data

(30)   Convention priority data

(40)   Date(s) of making available to the public

(50)   Technical information

(60)   Reference(s) to other legally related domestic document(s)

(70)   Identification of parties concerned with the document

(80)   Identification of data related to international conventions

There are more than 40 different codes in the list, of which the following are considered to be the minimum elements which should appear on the first page of a document and in an entry in an official gazette:

(11)   Number of the document

(12)   Plain-language designation of the kind of document

(21)   Number(s) assigned to the application(s)

(22)   Date(s) of filing application(s)

(23)   Other date(s) of filing, including exhibition date and date of filing complete specification following provisional specification

(31)   Number(s) assigned to priority application(s)

(32)   Date(s) of filing priority application(s)

(33)   Country (countries) in which priority application(s) was (were) filed

(51)   International Patent Classification

(54)   Title of invention

(61)   Domestic document(s) related by addition(s)

(62)   Domestic document(s) related by division(s)

(63)   Domestic document(s) related by continuation(s)

(64)   Domestic document(s) related by reissue(s)

A significant omission from the list of minimum elements, at least from an information searcher's point of view, is INID code (57), Abstract or claim.

Code (11), the number of the document, is of course the most frequently used shorthand method of citing a patent, and as it appears on the document it consists of three parts:

1.   Country code

2.   Patent number

3.   Status indicator

Country codes derive from International Standard 3166 Code for the representation of names of countries,[2] and each comprises two capital letters, as GB for Great Britain, CH for Switzerland, and so on. A list of patent offices which publish patent specifications, together with their country code letters, is given in Table 6.1.

The patent number is that allocated by the issuing authority, and customarily consists of seven digits. The status indicator, which varies from country to country, is based on work coordinated by the WIPO Permanent Committee on Patent Information (PCPI) in conjunction with issuing offices, and the sequence adopted by the European Patent Office is a good example of how the status of a patent is shown:

A1   European application (with search report)
A2   European application (without search report)

> A3   European application (search report for A2)
> B1   European patent
> B2   European revised patent

International Patent Classification (IPC)

One of the INID codes noted above is code (51): International Patent Classification, a reference to 'a system for the classification of patent specifications according to the inventions set out therein'. The IPC, which is covered by the Strasbourg Agreement of 24 March 1971, is administered

Table 6.1 List of Patent Offices which publish Patent Specifications and Country Code Letters

Argentine	AR	Japan	JP
African Region Industrial		Korea	KR
Property Office (ARIPO)	AP	Monaco	MC
Australia	AU	Netherlands	NL
Austria	AT	New Zealand	NZ
Belgium	BE	Norway	NO
Brazil	BR	Organisation Africaine de la	
Bulgaria	BG	Propriété Intellectuelle (OAPI)	OA
Canada	CA	Pakistan	PK
China	CN	Philippines	PH
Cuba	CU	Poland	PL
Czechoslovakia	CS	Portugal	PT
Denmark	DK	Romania	RO
Egypt	EG	South Africa	ZA
Eire	IE	Spain	ES
European Patent Office	EP	Sweden	SF
Finland	FI	Switzerland	CH
France	FR	United Kingdom	GB
Germany (DDR)	DD	United States of America	US
Germany (Federal Republic)	DE	Union of Soviet	
Hungary	HU	Socialist Republics	SU
Iceland	IS	Vietnam	VN
India	IN	World Intellectual Property	
Israel	IL	Organization (WIPO)	WO
Italy	IT	Yugoslavia	YU

*For arrangements since the reunification of Germany, see Chapter 5.

by WIPO, and 27 states are currently party to the agreement, although the IPC is actually used by the patent offices of some 70 countries.

The IPC divides technology into eight main sections and approximately 64 000 subdivisions. The sections A–H are virtually the same as the eight sections in the United Kingdom classification, but as the British Patent Office takes pains to point out, the principles upon which the IPC is based differ in some respects from those of the UK classification.

Although they are similar in overall structure, detailed coincidence between the two is not in general very pronounced. The broad outlines of the two schemes serve to indicate where some of the divergences occur.

IPC
A	Human necessities
B	Performing operations; transporting
C	Chemistry; metallurgy
D	Textiles; paper
E	Fixed constructions
F	Mechanical engineering; lighting; heating; weapons; blasting
G	Physics
H	Electricity

UK
A	Human necessities
B	Performing operations
C	Chemistry; metallurgy
D	Textiles; paper
E	Civil engineering; building accessories
F	Mechanics; lighting; heating
G	Instrumentation
H	Electricity

The UK's 'instrumentation' has become the IPC's broader 'physics', whilst the British 'civil engineering' has been turned into the less meaningful 'fixed constructions'. In the schedules themselves greater differences appear, and this point can be demonstrated by returning to the example of the peristaltic pump discussed in Chapter 4. The IPC treatment is as follows:

F04 – Positive displacement machines for liquids; pumps for liquids or elastic fluids

F04B – Positive displacement machines for liquids pumps

F04B 43/100 – Machines, pumps or pumping installations having flexible working members

43/12 – having peristaltic action

The term 'peristaltic' does not appear as a main entry in the official catchword index, but it can be found as a subheading under 'pumps'. In the case of the British classification key, the expression 'peristaltic devices' occurs as a main entry in the catchword index.

The IPC is regularly revised (the current revision period is every 5 years) and the 5th edition, which came into force in 1990, is indicated on the front page of a specification by the superscript numeral five, thus: Int.Cl^5. The earlier editions of the IPC were:

1st	1.9.68 – 30.6.74
2nd	1.7.74 – 31.12.79
3rd	1.1.80 – 31.12.84
4th	1.1.85 – 31.12.89

The IPC is published for WIPO in several volumes by Carl Heymanns Verlag, Munich, with the final volume of the set constituting a guide, survey of classes and summary of the main groups. The IPC is supplemented by the already mentioned catchword index, which is intended to indicate the part or parts of the schedules in which matter relating to any given subject is likely to be found, as indeed is the case with the British catchword index. A simple example of its usefulness is the facility for distinguishing between common terms having two or more separate meanings, as for example:

> Lighters   = barges
>   = devices for igniting

World Intellectual Property Organization

So far this chapter has considered two important international aspects of the patent system, namely the Patent Cooperation Treaty and the International Patent Classification. The common link between both is the World Intellectual Property Organization (WIPO) which administers them, and it is appropriate to examine the origins and role of WIPO in the context of patents as a source of information.

The World Intellectual Property Organization, referred to in its abbreviated form in English as WIPO, OMPI in French, and Spanish, and also in Russian, was established by a convention signed at Stockholm in 1967, entitled 'Convention Establishing the World Intellectual Property Organization'. The Convention came into force in 1970.

The origins of WIPO go back to 1883, the year of the adoption of the Paris Convention for the Protection of Industrial Property, and to 1886, the year of the adoption of the Berne Convention for the Protection of Literary and Artistic Works. Both conventions provided for the establishment of an international bureau or secretariat. These offices were united in 1893 and operated under a variety of names, the most recent being the United International Bureaux for the Protection of Intellectual Property, usually known as BIRPI, from the French version of the name.

In 1974 WIPO became one of the 16 specialized agencies of the United Nations.

The objectives of WIPO are twofold: firstly to promote the protection of intellectual property throughout the world through cooperation among states, and where appropriate, in collaboration with other international organizations; and secondly to ensure administrative cooperation among the intellectual property unions.

Intellectual property comprises two main branches:

1. Industrial property, mainly in inventions, trademarks and industrial designs, for which registration is required to established priority.
2. Copyright, chiefly literary, musical, artistic, photographic and audiovisual works, for which registration is not required in most countries.

WIPO promotes the protection of intellectual property by encouraging the conclusion of relevant international treaties, by giving assistance to developing countries, by assembling and disseminating information, and by maintaining facilities for the obtaining of protection. In terms of administrative cooperation, WIPO centralizes the work of the unions in the International Bureau in Geneva, with the aim of achieving economies for the member states. However, centralization is incomplete as far as copyright and neighbouring rights are concerned, since the Universal Copyright Convention is administered by the United Nations Educational Scientific and Cultural Organization (Unesco), and the administration of the Rome Convention on Neighbouring Rights is ensured by WIPO in cooperation with Unesco and the International Labour Office. The list of unions or treaties administered by WIPO in the field of industrial property is an extensive one, and runs (in chronological order of their creation) as follows:

1883 the Paris Union (for the protection of industrial property)

1891 the Madrid Agreement (for the repression of false or deceptive indications of sources of goods)

1891 the Madrid Union (for the international registration of trade marks)

1925 the Hague Agreement (for the international deposit of industrial designs)

1957 the Nice Union (for the international classification of goods and services for the purposes of the registration of marks)

1958 the Lisbon Agreement (for the protection of appellations of origin and their international registration)

1968 the Locarno Union (for the establishment of an international classification for industrial designs)

1970 the Patent Cooperation Treaty (noted above)

1971 the International Patent Classification Union (noted above)

1973 the Trademark Registration Treaty (for filing international applications for trademarks)

1973 the Vienna Agreement (for the establishment of an international classification of the figurative elements of marks)

1977 the Budapest Treaty (for the international recognition deposit of microorganisms for the purposes of procedure)

1981 the Nairobi Treaty (on the protection of the Olympic symbol).

In the field of copyright and neighbouring rights, the list runs:

1886 the Berne Union (for the protection of literary and artistic works)

1961 the Rome Convention (for the protection of performers, producers of phonograms and broadcasting organizations)

1971 the Geneva Convention (for the protection of the producers of phonograms against unauthorized duplication)

1974 the Brussels Convention (on the distribution of programme-carrying signals transmitted by satellite)

In addition, WIPO provides administration services for the International Union for the Protection of New Varieties of Plants (UPOV), concluded in Paris in 1961.

Three treaties, all adopted in 1989, will, once they come into effect, also be administered by WIPO, namely:

1. The IRAW Treaty for the international registration of audiovisual works

2. The IPIC Treaty for the protection of intellectual property in integrated circuits

3. The Madrid Protocol for the further development of the international registration of marks

The above list is a brief indication of the extremely wide range of WIPO activities, many of which of course are not connected with patents, but nevertheless include difficult areas of interest to information searchers, such as integrated circuits. On 1 January 1990, 126 states were party to the convention establishing WIPO.

Finally, mention must be made of WIPO and the International Patent

Documentation Centre (INPADOC). INPADOC was established in 1972 in Vienna, pursuant to an agreement between the Republic of Austria and WIPO, with the aim of establishing a bibliographical database, information from which can be retrieved for a variety of purposes by patent offices, industry and research and development establishments worldwide. The work of INPADOC, and its recent change in status, are discussed in Chapter 7.

Publications from WIPO

The World Intellectual Property Organization is a major publisher on topics of interest to those using patents as a source of information, quite apart from the regular periodicals which are considered in Chapter 7.

Some of their key publications are the monthly journal *Industrial Property*, the texts of conventions, treaties and agreements, the International Patent Classification (noted above), model laws and model provisions, and various commentaries, guides and studies. A complete catalogue is available from WIPO in Geneva.

References

1. Minimum documentation (1986) *PCT Gazette*, Section IV, 09/1986

2 *Codes for the representation of names of countries*, (1974) Geneva: Organisation International de Normalisation (ISO:3166).

CHAPTER SEVEN

Announcement and abstracting services

Introduction to announcement services

As has been noted earlier, the essence of a patent system is the reliance on priority dates, and as a consequence the official announcement journals issued by the various patent offices are scanned with an extraordinary degree of diligence by agents and information searchers alike, for such publications contain a wealth of detail on which companies are active in the patents area and the fields in which they are working.

This chapter concentrates on announcement services of the formal kind which aim to provide complete records on a regular basis. There are of course a number of publications which seek to disseminate information about new patents in a less formal, more selective and, in some cases, popularized manner, particularly for readers interested in patents as a source of information, and such items are examined in this chapter.

Some idea of the sheer scale of official publishing activities associated with patents (and by inference the problems presented to information searchers) can be gained by examining Rimmer's *International guide to official industrial property publications*,[1] which covers publications from over 50 patenting authorities throughout the world. The guide describes the official publications of each country, and includes details of utility models, designs and trademarks. Separate sections for each country contain a brief history of the legislation and procedures, current legislation, explanations of specifications, official gazettes and indexes, sources of reports of legal judgements, and early publications. The guide also gives information on international conventions and computer-based search systems.

Faced with such a flood of publications, only the largest of libraries can hope to maintain anything like a comprehensive collection. In the United Kingdom the task falls to the British Library Science, Reference and Information Service, which has compiled a *Guide to Industrial Property Holdings*.[2] This constitutes a location index to a collection comprising more than 30 million patent specifications, as well as abstracts and abridgments, official journals and gazettes, trademarks and designs from almost every issuing authority in the world. The collection itself is discussed more fully later in this chapter.

The size of the official output also necessitates a selective view when considering some of its characteristics and, as a result the approach in this present chapter has been to concentrate on the key publications from the various patenting authorities mentioned elsewhere in this book, namely the United Kingdom, the European system, WIPO, and the United States, Germany, Japan and Australia. In this way the salient features of particular importance to information searchers can be highlighted in a representative manner.

Practice, for example, varies with respect to the issue of official abstracts – in Great Britain they receive special treatment as separate series of publications, whilst in the United States it is the custom to publish in the *Official Gazette* one claim to show the scope of a specification. Whichever method is adopted for the publication of official abstracts or résumés of patents, the importance of such summaries in information work cannot be overstressed, because, as has been noted elsewhere, the titles given to patent specifications are often very poor indicators of the true subject matter. Moreover a well-prepared indicative abstract can often act as an eliminator, in the sense that it confirms that the invention disclosed, although relevant, is not pertinent to the enquiry in hand and so can safely be disregarded, or perhaps placed in a background file.

Official journals and gazettes

All countries which are signatories of the Paris Convention are obliged to publish what is termed 'an official periodical journal', providing details of granted patents and registered trademarks. In the case of the United Kingdom, details of British patents are published in the *Official Journal (Patents)*, a weekly periodical containing information on all United Kingdom applications filed, specifications published and patents granted, plus a statement of patents expired and patents ceased. The *Official Journal* provides a comprehensive record of all patents granted during a given week which have effect in the United Kingdom, and of all the applications made under the UK national patent law. No abstracts are included, and the seven-figure publication numbers are allocated so that they appear in order of classification headings when set out in numerical order.

With regard to British practice, it may be recalled that in discussing the *Classification Key*, mention was made (page 43) of the rearrangement of the 40 divisions into which the eight main sections of the scheme had been split, into 25 *Classification Key* units for the purpose of issuing abridgments and abstracts.

In the procedure under pre–1977 legislation, when an examiner dealt with an application he also prepared an abridgment summarizing the substance of the disclosure in the relevant specification. Where the specification included drawings, at least one was usually employed to illustrate the abridgment. The virtues of this arrangement were that the abridgments were of a uniform and high standard, because they were written by professionals.

Under the 1977 Act it is the applicant who is required to provide an abstract, which should identify the technical subject of the invention and the advance in that subject. In addition, the applicant is required to indicate which of any drawings he thinks should serve to illustrate the abstract. The examiner can reframe the abstract if he considers it appropriate, but he no longer prepares an old-style abridgment. The outcome is a wide variation in the quality of the abstracts compiled, as abstracting is an art which some applicants find hard to grasp.

Abstracts of specifications published under the 1977 Act appear weekly in pamphlet form, sorted into the above-mentioned 25 units of the *Classification Key* and arranged in serial order within each unit. Periodically, all the pamphlets of each unit are collected into a volume, and each such volume includes the relevant unit of the *Classification Key* in force during the relevant period, plus a subject index based on the key and an index of applicants' names. Volumes are made available as soon as possible after the end of each annual series, and include both abridgments published under the 1949 Act (and now of course getting rarer and rarer) and abstracts published under the new Act.

Abstracts and abridgments can be studied in major libraries, and they can also be obtained on subscription in order to build up collections in specific subject areas for use in industrial property offices and company libraries. When scanned on a regular basis they offer a valuable and reliable current awareness service, and contain sufficent information to enable searchers to make a decision on whether or not to consult a specification in full. As a retrospective aid, abstracts and abridgments allow a rapid and systematic assessment of specifications identified as a result of requests for file lists, and are an effective means of narrowing a long list of potentially relevant items to the few which are really crucial to an enquirer's needs.

European Patent Office

The European Patent Office publishes a weekly *European Patent Bulletin*, each issue of which is in two parts: I – Published European patent applications and international applications, and II – Granted patents. Bibliographical entries are identified by INID numbers, and titles are provided in the three official languages, but no abstracts are appended. The *European Patent Bulletin* may be regarded as the equivalent of the British *Official Journal (Patents)*, but the EPO also has its own *Official Journal*, which is again trilingual and carries general information and announcements from the President of the EPO, grouped under the following regular headings: Administrative Council; Decisions of the Boards of Appeal; Legal advice and information from the EPO; Representation; Information from the contracting states; Vacancies; and Fees. This publication appears monthly.

Between 1978 and 1984, abstracts were available as *European Patent Office – Classified Abstracts*, weekly issues of abstracts of European published applications, bound annually in International Patent Classification order. Nowadays the Munich publishers Wila Verlag (Wilhelm Lampl KG) have the task of issuing abstracts of European patent documents under the title *Auszüge aus den Europaischen Patentanmeldungen* (EPZ). This appears weekly in three parts, and contains abstracts from the European Patent Office arranged by the IPC. Part 1 covers basic and raw materials industries, chemistry and metalworking, building and mining; Part 2 deals with electrochemistry, physics, mechanics, optics and acoustics; and Part 3 includes remaining process industries and manufacturing methods, machines and vehicle construction, nutrition and agriculture.

Each entry provides bibliographic details, main claims and a drawing, in a layout identified by INID numbers. The length of the abstract varies considerably and the language is that of the application (i.e. English French or German). A further weekly publication, *Auszüge aus den Europaischen Patentschriften* provides (in German) complete bibliographic data, the most important claim and the most important drawing for all granted European patents. In cooperation with the Bertelsmann Information Service, Wila Verlag also provides the online database PATOS, which contains information on more than 2.3 million patents from Germany, Europe and those applied for under the Patent Cooperation Treaty.

Patent Cooperation Treaty

The announcement service of World Intellectual Property Organization is the *PCT Gazette: Gazette of International Patent Applications*, an official publication under the patent cooperation treaty which has appeared every second week since 1978. In addition to the regular issues, at least two issues per year are reserved for notices and information of a general character. However, the bulk of the *PCT Gazette* is devoted to abstracts of PCT applications, which are presented in a compact format allowing two applications per page, arranged by WO numbers. In addition, WIPO publishes pamphlets identified again by WO, followed by the last two digits of the year and a unique five-digit number, e.g. WO 78/00001. The pamphlets contain the text of the application, an abstract and an international search report, and are available according to categories within the International Patent Classification. Typical PCT abstracts are shown in Figure 7.1.

United States

In the United States the *Official Gazette of the United States Patent and Trademark Office* is published each week, with details of patents granted, including summaries and drawings, arranged in three groups: General and mechanical, chemical, and electrical. *The Official Gazette* provides a summary of each item by reproducing in full one claim (in most cases the first claim), with an indication of the total number of claims in the specification. The inclusion of a claim accounts for the enormous bulk of the *Official Gazette*, each, annual volume of which occupies several feet of shelving. Patents are listed in numerical order but the patent numbers are assigned in such a way that they will appear in the order of the US classification system.

The *Official Gazette* is supplemented by an *Index of Patents Issued...*, which comes out on an annual basis and is divided into two parts: I: List of patentees with brief subject indication; II: Index of subjects of inventions. The *Index* is arranged in numerical order, by class numbers taken from the US classification.

Germany

In the Federal Republic of Germany the Deutsches Patentamt compiles and issues the official journal *Patentblatt*, containing details of applications, granted patents, utility models, and European and PCT applications. Extracts from German patent documents (bibliographic details, main claim and the most important drawing) are published on a weekly basis by Wila Verlag in a format similar to that for EPO patents, and in the same three parts as noted above. In the case of applications the title is *Auszüge aus den Offenlegungsschriften*; for granted patents, *Auszüge aus den Patentschriften*, whilst for utility models, the title is *Auszüge aus den Gebrauchsmustern*.

Japan

The Japanese Patent Office publishes four official gazettes, namely:

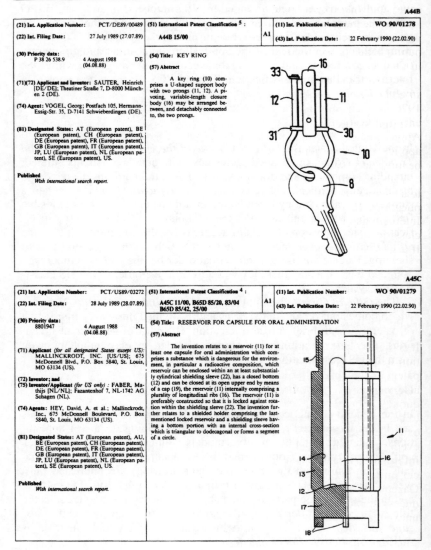

A44B

(21) Int. Application Number: PCT/DE89/00489	(51) International Patent Classification [5] :		(11) Int. Publication Number: WO 90/01278
(22) Int. Filing Date: 27 July 1989 (27.07.89)	A44B 15/00	A1	(43) Int. Publication Date: 22 February 1990 (22.02.90)

(30) Priority data:
    P 38 26 538.9   4 August 1988   DE
                  (04.08.88)

(71)(72) Applicant and Inventor: SAUTER, Heinrich [DE/DE]; Theatiner Straße 7, D-8000 München 2 (DE).

(74) Agent: VOGEL, Georg; Postfach 105, Hermann-Essig-Str. 35, D-7141 Schwieberdingen (DE).

(81) Designated States: AT (European patent), BE (European patent), CH (European patent), DE (European patent), FR (European patent), GB (European patent), IT (European patent), JP, LU (European patent), NL (European patent), SE (European patent), US.

Published
    With international search report.

(54) Title: KEY RING

(57) Abstract

    A key ring (10) comprises a U-shaped support body with two prongs (11, 12). A pivoting, variable-length closure body (16) may be arranged between, and detachably connected to, the two prongs.

A45C

(21) Int. Application Number: PCT/US89/03272	(51) International Patent Classification [4] :		(11) Int. Publication Number: WO 90/01279
(22) Int. Filing Date: 28 July 1989 (28.07.89)	A45C 11/00, B65D 85/20, 83/04 B65D 85/42, 25/00	A1	(43) Int. Publication Date: 22 February 1990 (22.02.90)

(30) Priority data:
    8801947   4 August 1988   NL
                (04.08.88)

(71) Applicant *(for all designated States except US):* MALLINCKRODT, INC. [US/US]; 675 McDonnell Blvd., P.O. Box 5840, St. Louis, MO 63134 (US).

(72) Inventor; and
(75) Inventor/Applicant *(for US only)* : FABER, Mathijs [NL/NL]; Fazantenhof 7, NL-1742 AG Schagen (NL).

(74) Agents: HEY, David, A. et al.; Mallinckrodt, Inc., 675 McDonnell Boulevard, P.O. Box 5840, St. Louis, MO 63134 (US).

(81) Designated States: AT (European patent), AU, BE (European patent), CH (European patent), DE (European patent), FR (European patent), GB (European patent), IT (European patent), JP, LU (European patent), NL (European patent), SE (European patent), US.

Published
    With international search report.

(54) Title: RESERVOIR FOR CAPSULE FOR ORAL ADMINISTRATION

(57) Abstract

    The invention relates to a reservoir (11) for at least one capsule for oral administration which comprises a substance which is dangerous for the environment, in particular a radioactive composition, which reservoir can be enclosed within an at least substantially cylindrical shielding sleeve (22), has a closed bottom (12) and can be closed at its open upper end by means of a cap (19), the reservoir (11) internally comprising a plurality of longitudinal ribs (16). The reservoir (11) is preferably constructed so that it is locked against rotation within the shielding sleeve (22). The invention further relates to a shielded holder comprising the last-mentioned locked reservoir and a shielding sleeve having a bottom portion with an internal cross-section which is triangular to dodecagonal or forms a segment of a circle.

Figure 7.1   Typical abstracts from the *PCT Gazette*, (with acknowledgements to WIPO)

Kokai Tokkyo Koho (Patent Application Gazette); *Tokkyo Koho* (Patent Gazette); *Kokai Jitsuyo Shin An Koho* (Utility Model Application Gazette), and *Jitsuyo Shin An Koho* (Utility Model Gazette).

The sheer volume of output is a librarian's nightmare, with up to six volumes in each of the four series appearing daily except on Sundays and public holidays, a consequence of course of the tremendous activity noted in Chapter 5.

Access for non-Japanese speakers is made possible through *Patent Abstracts of Japan*, published in English by the Japanese Patent Office since 1976, with an emphasis on technical fields where a high incidence of patent applications between Japan and foreign countries exists. Approximately half the total output of patent applications is covered, but applications from non-residents are excluded on the basis that they will be more accessible in another language in the country of origin.

Patent Abstracts of Japan contains English-language abstracts, three to a page, with drawings where appropriate, of published unexamined applications in four main fields, each of which embraces a number of International Patent Classification subclasses. (The domestic Japanese classification had 136 main classes but was abandoned in favour of the IPC in 1980). The four fields are:

M: General and mechanical

C: Chemical

E: Electrical

P: Physics

It is quite common for Japanese patents abstracts, rather than the application documents themselves, to be quoted on the front pages of western patent documents under INID code (56): List of prior art documents. It is also the practice of some Japanese inventors applying for full patents to quote within the text details from applications for utility models, in order to demonstrate the disadvantages inherent in current technology. See, for example, DE 4024189 on air bags to protect vehicle occupants in the event of a crash, which refers to utility model 861/89. English-language information about Japanese patents is coordinated through the Japan Patent Information Organization (JAPIO), which supplies copies of Official Gazettes or translations of extracts from them. In addition, JAPIO produces a monthly index service on COM-microfiche for Japanese unexamined applications, available as:

JPIN Document number

JPIA Applicant name

JPIC International Patent Classification

The JAPIO indexes can be used via INPADOC, which also provides access to Japanese patent information on the database PATOLIS, using a Kanji Terminal Emulator for online searching (see Figure 7.2).

Abstracts of Japanese patents are also available through Derwent, the services of which, together with those of INPADOC, are examined later in this chapter. However, it is worth drawing attention to the Derwent output at this particular juncture in order to mention the scope of the coverage. Abstracts of Japanese material in the single-country bulletin section of *World Patent Index* are confined to items placed under headings A–M of the Derwent Classification, and thus the Derwent title *Japanese Patents Abstracts* covers unexamined and examined applications in the chemical field only. Japanese patents are also covered in the alerting abstract bulletins derived from the *Chemical Patents Index* and the *Electrical Patents Index*, but not the *General and Mechanical Patents Index*.

In Great Britain the British Library Science Reference and Information Service has special resources to deal with all types of Japanese publications (not just patents), and linguistic help is available through its Japanese Information Service (JIS). The SRIS collection contains more than 9 000 000 Japanese patents and virtually all Japanese industrial property publications.

```
***  DcResult  ***  [P&Ut] Form(C) OrderNo:(99999999)  88.10.14    No.: 0000001
***  ex. P 60- 59283  [60.12.24] Req. (1) ***
App.  57-232557 [57.12.27] uPub 59-118805 [59.07.09] Reg.  1332342 [61.08.14]
Tit. ex:  不活性ガス連続金属噴霧装置
sSum      〔目的〕特定構造の噴霧タンクに、金属粉末と不活性ガスを分離して各々
          を回収する手段を接続して密閉構造としてなる、金属粉末を生産性よく且
          つ連続的に製造できる装置。
Keywords: 不活性 ガス 連続 金属 噴霧, タンク, 粉末, 分離, 回収, 密閉 構
          造, 溶解炉
Appnt ex: 132000227 SUMITOMO KEIKINZOKU KOGYO KK
Invtr:    犬丸 晋, 渋江 和久
Prio.:
Unx  IPC:  *B22F  9/08 .
Ex   IPC:  *B22F  9/08 .
Ex   JPC:  *          . .
JCl:    125 (R031)
Agent       norm  (7819)  Ot(2)   Appnt # (01)   Inv. # (01)   Prio. # (00)
Kd App.    (norm)       Or. App. No. ( - )        Or. Reg. No. (      )
Bas Dt (App. Dt )  [57.12.27]  RactDt [ . . ]  Sect (3-4)  PAGE # (0006)
Right transfer ( )    Enforcem. Cons. ( )
Rel. App.
Opp. # (00)  Kd Dec. (Reg.) [61.05.27]    Fin. Dec. (Reg.    ) [61.08.14]
ExamType (NormExam) ( -    ) [ . . ] TrDe    ( ) [ . . ]
PRS INFO             (PRS Code81, 600105, 38300) (PRS Code15, 601008, 7518 )
81  Request for Examination
15  Decision of Publication
 (PRS Code35, 610328, 7518 ) (PRS CodeA1, 610527, 7518 ) (Reg. Fee: 61, 610603, 00000)
35  Sending back (no Opposition to Publication)
A1  Decision of Registration
61  Payment of Registration Fee
   Cit. Ref:
```

Figure 7.2   Sample of INPADOC Kanji emulator translation (with acknowledgements to INPADOC)

Australia

The *Australian Official Journal of Patents* contains, in addition to the customary records and official notices, patent abridgments of accepted complete specifications. A *Supplement* to the *Official Journal* carries abstracts of specifications open to public inspection.

Although the Australian system has its origins in the British system (even down to the spelling of the word 'abridgment'), Australia maintains a dual identification for summaries, consisting of the term Abstracts for applications (the AU-A document) and the term Abridgments for granted patents (the AU-B document).

As already noted, the inventor is not required to prepare a summary of his invention, and in practice the text in the *Official Journal* is that of the first, or most significant, claim. In consequence, the abstract and the abridgment for the same specification may differ if the claims have been subject to any amendment during processing.

Abstracting and indexing services

As noted in Chapter 6, the International Patent Documentation Centre (INPADOC) was founded in 1972 following an agreement between WIPO and the Republic of Austria. INPADOC was set up as a limited liability company (Gesellschaft mit beschränkter Haftung GmbH), and until 1990 was fully owned by the Austrian government. In 1991, ownership was transferred to the European Patent Office, but the treaty of transfer specified that the information departments would remain in Vienna.

INPADOC's function is to record, by means of a huge computer database, the bibliographic details of patents as soon as possible after they become available to the public. The files so created contain information on more than 15 million patent documents, which is made available in the form of various services noted below. Currently INPADOC indexes patents from over 50 countries, supplemented by data from the European Patent Office and the International Bureau of WIPO. Some of the information available through INPADOC dates back to 1920 and earlier, but the bulk of the data has been accumulated since 1973, with some backfiles extending to 1968.

INPADOC acquires its information from a variety of sources, principally magnetic tape files provided by individual national patent offices, but also the patent documents themselves, and official gazettes. The following items of bibliographic information are recorded for each specification:

● Country or office of publication

- Publication number and date
- Priority details
- Application details
- International Patent Classification number(s)
- Applicant(s)
- Inventor(s)
- Title

These details are held on a database which can be accessed online (see Chapter 9) or manually through a series of indexes produced in COM microfiche format, namely:

- NDB Numerical Data Base
- PCS Patent Classification Service
- PAS Patent Applicant Service by IPC symbols
- PAP Patent Applicant Service by priorities
- PIS Patent Inventor Service
- PRS Patent Register Service

The NDB provides a complete record of bibliographic data – the publication details, application and priority information, IPC classification, applicant, inventor and title – in numerical order, whereas the PCS lists the patent documents according to the IPC symbols allotted to them by the various patent offices. In the PAS, patent documents in the name of the same applicant are grouped according to the IPC main coding, enabling the user to find all the technical fields in which a company or an inventor is active. The PAP, on the other hand, provides under each applicant's name a list of patent documents by priority date, and offers an easy way of finding non-priority supplementary applications relating to a specific patent family.

The PIS pinpoints inventors as individuals, and is a means of monitoring the output of experts and specialists over a given period, as well as charting their movements from one organization to another. The findings can be cross-checked with indexes to the published literature, where the inventors may also appear as authors or co-authors of technical papers.

PRS constitutes an important time-saver in that it provides regular information on the legal status of patents, in particular, confirmation that individual specifications are still in force. It also notes cancellations, declarations of nullity, withdrawals and refusals.

INPADOC also offers a Patent Family Service (PFS) which brings together patent publications based on at least one common priority claim – the sorting key is the priority country, and within the priority country it is the priority date, the kind of priority application and its number. PFS can be combined with a further service, the INPADOC Numerical List (INL) wherein families are sorted according to priority numbers and within each priority number by priority date.

Whereas all the above services give access to the database via a specific feature, INPADOC also compiles a journal of record in the form of its *INPADOC Patent Gazette*, which records on a weekly basis bibliographic data relating to all the patent documents processed during the relevant 7 days. The *Gazette* constitutes a monitoring and current-awareness service of enormous scope, and consists of four parts:

- Selected Numerical Service (SNS)
- Selected Classification Service (SCS)
- Selected Applicant Service (SAS)
- Selected Inventor Service (SIS)

Other services provided by INPADOC include the answering of individual requests for information, the operation of online services, access to the files of the Japanese Patent Information Organization (JAPIO), and the CAPRI system.

The CAPRI system (Computerized Adminstration of Patent Documents Reclassified According to the IPC) covers patent documents issued from at least 1920 until the end of 1972, by Germany, France, Japan, the Soviet Union, Switzerland, the UK and the USA. Information relating to the country of publication, document number, kind of document, IPC symbols, and the edition in which the IPC symbol is valid, is being processed by INPADOC to create a central database (CDB) listing patents by IPC symbols, and a central inverted file (CIF) listing the same documents by country of origin and document number.

The sheer size and range of INPADOC's activities serve to emphasize, firstly the magnitude of the world's inventiveness as represented by the continuous flood of patent documents, and secondly, the control measures which have to be taken to impose some sort of coherence on the ways the information can be accessed. Yet despite this tremendous expenditure of effort, the INPADOC files do not mean the end of the road as far as the information searcher is concerned, for the one vital element the INPADOC records lack is an abstract or an abridgment. In other words, INPADOC provides the bibliographic means for identification, but for the purposes of evaluation and appraisal it is necessary to consult sources which supply abstracts.

Of such services, those provided by the Derwent Company are by far the most comprehensive. The origins of Derwent Publications Limited, which is now part of the Thomson Organization, have been described by Oppenheim,[3] and further summarized by Eisenschitz.[4] From very modest beginnings, the output of Derwent has grown to embrace five main printed services, backed by the World Patent Index online databases. These individual services are:

- Chemical Patents Index (CPI)
- Electrical Patents Index (EPI)
- General and Mechanical Patents Index (GMPI)
- World Patents Abstracts (WPA)
- World Patents Index Gazette Service (WPI)

CPI began in 1971 and currently processes about 7000 patents per week, from 31 patent-issuing authorities. Alerting bulletins are available for the twelve sections of CPI, namely:

A Plastics, polymers

B Pharmaceuticals

C Agricultural chemicals

D Food; detergents

E General chemicals

F Textiles; paper

G Printing; coating; photographic

H Petroleum

J Chemical engineering

K Nucleonics; explosives

L Refractories; ceramics; electrochemistry

M Metallurgy

In addition, the CPI service provides a second type of abstract, the documentation abstract, which contains much extra detail and is designed to be the prime source of reference for retrospective searching. Documentation Abstracts are unique to the CPI service.

EPI started in 1980 and covers about 4300 patents per week, again from 31 patent-issuing authorities. It is split into six sections, thus:

S Measuring; testing

T Computing and control

U Semiconductors and circuitry

V Electronic components

W Communications

X Electric power engineering

The GMPI service covers general and mechanical technology, bridging the gap between CPI and EPI. Thirty-patent issuing offices are monitored and there are four titles:

P1–P3 Human necessities P4-P8 Performing operations
Q1–Q4 Transport, construction
Q5-Q7 Mechanical engineering

World Patent Abstracts constitutes a series of publications devoted to single countries, and for a given country, where the output is large, the title is divided into a number of editions based on subject categories. The titles are:

- Belgian Patents Abstracts
- British Patents Abstracts
- European Patents Abstracts
- French Patents Abstracts (includes South Africa)
- German Patents Abstracts
- Japanese Patents Abstracts
- Netherlands Patents Abstracts
- PCT Patents Abstracts
- Soviet Patents Abstracts
- United States Patents Abstracts

In all, some 14 500 abstracts are processed each week, no mean feat of coordination. The strength of the Derwent system lies in the use of abstractors skilled in both the technical subject and the language of publication. There are precise guidelines as to the length of an abstract, and in particular, contributors are enjoined to provide for each patent.

- A meaningful two-part title
- A succinct account of the invention claimed
- An indication of its field of use and the advantages it offers
- An indication of the diagram most likely to prove helpful in understanding the invention. A typical abstract is shown in Figure 7.3.

The abstracts are also used as input to create the database file, *World Patents Index*, which consists of two online files; WPI, which covers patent families with basic patents published in the years 1963–1980, and WPI/L (meaning WPI Latest) which covers families whose basic patent has been published in the period 1981 to date.

In addition to *World Patents Abstracts* and *World Patents Index*, Derwent offers a number of other publications of special interest to the

TOLG ★   **Q67**   89-062597/09   ★ **EP -304-914-A**
Lining pipelines by evagination technique - using compressed air as pressuring fluid to drive lining with water used as seal
    TOKYO GAS KK (ASHO) 26.08.87-JP-212464
    W01 X12 (01.03.89) F16l-58/10
25.08.88 as 113871 (1949RT) (E) US4064211 GB2071804 R(DE FR GB)
Compressed air is used as the pressurising fluid driving the lining (4) forward ano forcing the lining against the pipe to ensure a good bond.
  A liquid such as water is used in the pressure container (3B) to seal the air in the induction pipe (3A), the lining being pulled down through the water seal. The speed of the lining process is controlled by the endless belts (10).
    USE/ADVANTAGE - For telecommunication or power cable. Overcomes problems of sealing mechanically which   squeezed binder backwards as lining progressed and obviates water clearance and pressure differentials of wet systems. (11pp Dwg.No.1/4)
N89-047773

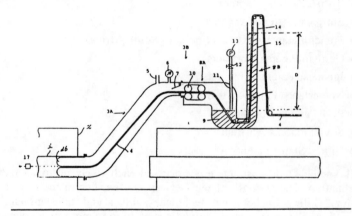

Figure 7.3   Example of a Derwent abstract (with acknowledgements to Derwent Publications)

information user, including newsletters, customised bulletins and patents profiles.

Also in the Derwent series, the *WPI Gazette Service* is produced as a low cost, abbreviated patents information service. It contains no abstracts and is issued in four weekly parts:

● General (P)

● Mechanical (Q)

● Electrical (R)

● Chemical (Ch)

Customized bulletins are tailor-made publications compiled in response to parameters specified by Derwent customers. The contents are confidential to the commissioning organization, but many customers eventually give permission for specific titles to be made more widely available, as for example in the field of electrophotography.

Patents profiles, on the other hand, take a broader approach and are not confidential. They constitute an alerting service covering the most up-to-date patents which are relevant to research-intensive industries and technologies, and take the form of regular bulletins covering relatively wide areas such as engineering, aerospace, medical devices, packaging and machine tools, which are subdivided into the specific, much narrower topics represented by the individual patents profiles, as for example vehicle tyres, aircraft weapon systems, diagnostics, films and foils, and welding. Such profiles are very useful where developments in limited, mutually exclusive areas are under regular scrutiny.

In essence, it can be seen that, taken together, the services provided by Derwent and INPADOC are to some extent complementary, both with each other and with official searching aids. They both have advantages over the official publications in that they allow searches of more than one country at a time, and because their cumulated indexes are often produced faster and cover greater periods of time than the official publications. Indeed, since some countries do not produce indexes themselves, the only practical method of searching is via INPADOC and/or Derwent.

References

1. Rimmer, B. (1988) *International guide to official industrial property publications*, 2nd edn. London: British Library, Science Reference and Information Service (SRIS), with 1990 update
2. *Guide to industrial property holdings* (1990). London: British Library; Science Reference and Information Service (SRIS)
3. Oppenheim, C. (1981) The patent services of Derwent Publications. *Science and Technology Libraries*, **2**, (2), 23–31
4. Eisenschitz, T.S. (1987) *Patents trade marks and designs in information work*. London: Croom Helm

CHAPTER EIGHT

Availability of information about patents

Introduction

The very success of the patent system and its adoption around the world has created considerable problems in accessibility and availability. Each issuing office naturally takes care to maintain a file of all its own publications, and the citizens of most countries have reasonable access to their national collections, but although patents are based on territorial rights, the need to be able to compare and evaluate ideas across national boundaries, especially by information searchers, means that to be worthwhile, collections must be international in character and scope.

Moreover, the information provided by announcement and abstracting services (discussed in Chapter 7) and the data made available by online searching systems (described in Chapter 9) mean that relevant patents from whatever country can be quickly and accurately identified, and, in consequence, create increased pressure for the prompt delivery of full texts.

The number of patent documents issued now runs to many millions, and whilst it is true that just as with the conventional literature there is a natural falling-off in the degree of usefulness (and hence demand) as the material grows older, researchers still need, on occasion, to delve very deeply into the distant past. Old notions, sometimes the subject of patents long in obscurity, have a habit of resurfacing in ways which embody known concepts in new guises. Past files are full of ideas developed before their time – sound inventions incapable of proper exploitation when originally conceived, perhaps because of the lack of a suitable material or an efficient power source. In many searches the need to take the long view is paramount.

At this juncture, too, the point needs to be reemphasized that the expression 'availability' is used in the sense that the information disclosed in a published application or a granted patent is available for public inspection and appraisal. It is not necessarily available for public *exploitation*, unless, in the case of a granted patent, the patent has been allowed to lapse through the non-payment of renewal fees. In addition, of course, the use of such information depends on other existing rights not being infringed.

A comprehensive review of the many sources of supply for published patent specifications, including patent offices (both national and international), regional suboffices, national technical libraries, depository centres, and various private sector services, can be found in the survey by Hill.[1]

Collections and networks

The specialized nature of patents literature is evidenced by the establishment in the UK of a Patents Information Network (PIN), the history of the development of which has been comprehensively reviewed by Newton.[2] In 1990, a total of 14 libraries held collections of varying degrees of completeness, with the coordinating role being fulfilled by the British Library. The object is to rationalize expenditure on a resource which is expensive to maintain, in terms both of expert staff and valuable storage space, and which, it has to be said, in many parts of the country is not greatly in demand. The result is a network comprising libraries in the following locations shown in Figure 8.1 (as at Summer 1991).

Access to the PIN collections is achieved with a minimum of formality; in the case of the Birmingham collection, for example, a special section of the city's reference library has been set aside exclusively for the users of patent literature. Readers may, on making themselves known to the staff, be afforded direct access to the stack. Experience has shown that such collections are regularly used by a small but knowledgeable clientele, often acting as intermediaries on behalf of a wider but less experienced cross-section of end-users, sometimes in a freelance capacity.

The make-up of the collections in the PIN varies from library to library. The heart of the network is the collection maintained by the British Library Science Reference and Information Service (SRIS), which consists of more than 30 million patent specifications, as well as abstracts and abridgments, official journals and gazettes. SRIS incorporates the former Patent Office Library, founded by Bennet Woodcroft and opened in 1855 as the Free Library of the Commissioner of Patents.[3] Holdings

P|A|T|E|N|T|S
INFORMATION NETWORK

ABERDEEN
0224 636811
Business & Technical Dept.
Central Library
Rosemount Viaduct
Aberdeen AB9 1GU

BELFAST
0232 243233
Patents Section
Central Library
Belfast Public Libraries
Royal Avenue
Belfast BT1 1EA

BIRMINGHAM
021-235 4537
Patents Department
Central Library
Chamberlain Square
Birmingham B3 3HQ

BRISTOL
0272 299148
Commercial Library
Central Library
College Green
Bristol BS1 5TL

COVENTRY
0203 838448
Lanchester Library
Coventry Polytechnic
Much Park Street
Coventry CV1 2HF

GLASGOW
041-221 7030
Patents Collection
Mitchell Library
North Street
Glasgow G3 7DN

LEEDS
0532 488747
Patents Information Unit
32 York Road
Leeds LS9 8TD

LIVERPOOL
051-225 5442
Patents Department
Central Library
William Brown Street
Liverpool L3 8EW

LONDON
071-323 7919
British Library
25 Southampton Buildings
Chancery Lane WC2A 1AW

MANCHESTER
061-236 9422
Patents Department
Central Library
St Peter's Square
Manchester M2 5PD

NEWCASTLE-UPON-TYNE
091 261 0691
Central Library
Princess Square
Newcastle-Upon-Tyne
NE99 1DX

PLYMOUTH
0752 264675
Reference Department
Central Library
Drake Circus
Plymouth PL4 8AL

PORTSMOUTH
0705 819311
Central Library
Guildhall Square
Portsmouth PO1 2DX

SHEFFIELD
0742 734742
Science & Technology Library
Central Library
Surrey Street
Sheffield S1 1XZ

Figure 8.1   Patents Information Network

range from Great Britain's earliest specifications, numbers 1–364, which appeared between 1617 and 1699, to those of the most recent major entrant on the patents scene, the Republic of China, with applications dating from 1985. The key to the collection, as mentioned in Chapter 7 is the *Guide to Industrial Property Holdings*,[4] which contains information on the holdings and shelf locations of publications from almost 100 offices, plus details of major reference books and periodicals on industrial property.

The resources of the library are backed by help from experienced staff, who regularly participate in seminars and courses on various practical aspects of patents information, such as the gleaning of commercial intelligence from patents and the techniques of online patents searching. In addition the British Library operates a photocopy delivery and online searching service called Patent Express, details of which are regularly reported in *Patent Express Newsletter*.

General current awareness is also provided by means of pages or columns in which patents are highlighted and discussed on a selective basis, in publications aimed at a wide but informed readership.

A further British Library service is called *Currentscan*, a regular watch on the patent literature arising as a result of activities under the European Patent Convention and the Patent Cooperation Treaty, and that emanating from the British Patent Office, plus other major countries as required. Customers of *Currentscan* can opt for a basic service, in which a watch is kept on any subject area defined in terms of the International Patent Classification, on up to 10 companies for a period of a year.

Resources in the libraries making up the PIN system outside London are not as comprehensive as those provided by the British Library, but are nevertheless very considerable. Taking once again the example of Birmingham, the city offers access to British patents back to 1884, US patents back to 1926, and those from the European Patent Office back to 1978.

The collection at another network library, Leeds, goes back even further (Great Britain to 1617, the United States to 1894). The Patent Information Unit run by Leeds City Council has a collection of 15 million British foreign patent documents, and can offer a photocopy supply service covering the following countries and authorities:

● Australia
● Belgium
● Canada
● Switzerland
● Germany (DE & DD)
● EPO
● France

- United Kingdom
- Netherlands
- United States
- PCT

The service is very rapid in response, very reliable and very widely used, with regular customers taking advantage of a deposit account facility.

Many libraries, and the industrial property departments of large commercial and manufacturing organizations, combine access to document delivery services such as those provided by Leeds and by SRIS, with direct subscriptions to the many microform files available through the Rapid Patent Service operated by Research Publications Inc. The full texts of the patent publications of around a dozen major patenting authorities, including the United Kingdom, the United States, the EPO and the PCT, are available on 16 mm microfilm, and greatly relieve the problems of shelf-space shortages, whilst ensuring absolute file integrity.

An important channel of communication, both for the organizers and the users of the Patent Information Network, is the newsletter *Patents Information News*, published quarterly by the British Library and edited in such a way that it emphasizes not only the scope of information contained in patents, but also its intrinsic interest and wide variety. Thus articles regularly appear on topics ranging from tennis rackets to vacuum cleaners, and from space shuttles to combs for killing fleas in cats' fur. The aim seems to be to stress the value of patents as technology development indicators, and also to dispel the notion that such information sources lack a broad appeal.

The Patents Information Network represents a concerted effort to make sure an information source rich in original ideas is fully appreciated and exploited, but the take-up rate is crucially dependent on the industrial health of the geographical regions in which the participating libraries are situated. In the case of the Midlands, a decline in the fortunes of manufacturing industry has led to the disappearance of many famous names, and has resulted in a corresponding drop in the use made of the locally organized collections. Another influencing factor has been the concentration of product support teams in purpose-built technical centres in other parts of the country, and in the case of firms which have been taken into foreign ownership, to locations abroad. Such teams contain people who regularly generate new ideas of their own, and need to compare them with developments patented by others.

Plans are in hand to extend the reach of the PIN by inviting a wide range of libraries, information and advice centres to join as Patent Gateways. The object is to raise awareness of patents among information providers in commercial, academic and research establishments, enabling them to direct enquirers who could profit from patents information to known contacts in the PIN.

Gateways will be provided with a portfolio of documentation covering the basic principles of patents information, and will be kept in touch with patent information activities both locally and nationally.

Great Britain is not the only country to recognize the need to make sources of information about patents available on a local basis, and initiatives similar to, although not identical with, the Patent Information Network can be found, for example in the United States, France, Australia and Germany.

In the United States, in addition to the national facilities provided by the Public Search Room of the Patent and Trademark Office in Arlington, Virginia, which are complemented by the Files Information Unit and backed up by the P&TO Scientific Library, the public across the nation has access to more than 60 collections which were originally designated Patent Depository Libraries (PDLs), and then renamed Patent and Trademark Depository Libraries.

PDLs receive current issues of United States patents and maintain collections of earlier issued patents. The scope of the collections varies from location to location, and ranges from recent patents to all or most of the patents issued since 1970. The collections, with the exception of that at the Patent Information Clearinghouse in Sunnyvale, California, which is arranged by subject matter, are organized in patent-number sequence, and are available for consultation by the public free of charge. Users also have access to the *Manual of Classification, Index to the US Patent Classification,* and *Classification Definitions.* Expert staff are on hand to aid the public in gaining effective access to the information contained in patents, and the Classification and Search Support Information System (CASSIS), which provides direct online access to Patent Office data, is available at all the depository libraries, and at some locations in Great Britain. (See Table 8.1 for a list of Patent Depository Libraries.)

In France, the network of the Institut National de la Propriété Industrielle (INPI) regional centres in Bordeaux, Lyon, Marseille, Nancy, Nice, Rennes and Strasbourg, is supplemented by a selected group of Agence Régionale d'Information Scientifique et Technique (ARIST) centres at Besançon, Dijon, Lille, Montpellier, Nantes and Toulouse, two university libraries (Caen and Clermont Ferrand) and four archive centres (Belfort, Grenoble, Rouen and Tarbes).

In Germany, public access to patent collections is provided at the Deutsches Patentamt in Munich, at its suboffice in Berlin, and at Patentauslegestellen (depository centres), eight of which, namely those at Aachen, Bochum, Darmstadt, Dortmund, Hamburg, Kaiserlautern, Nurnberg and Stuttgart, hold substantially complete sets of German patents. A further six centres hold partial sets based on subject interests. In the for-

Table 8.1 Reference collection of US patents available for public use in patent Depository Libraries

Alabama	Auburn University Libraries	(205) 844-7747
	Birmingham Public Library	(205) 226-3680
Alaska	Anchorage Municipal Libraries	(907) 261-2916
Arizona	Tempe: Noble Library, Arizona State University	(602) 965-7607
Arkansas	Little Rock: Arkansas State Library	(501) 682-2053
California	Los Angeles Public Library	(213) 612-3273
	Sacramento: California State Library	(916) 322-4572
	San Diego Public Library	(619) 236-5813
	Sunnyvale: Patent information Clearinghouse	(408) 730-7290
Colorado	Denver Public Library	(303) 571-2347
Connecticut	New Haven: Science Park Library	(203) 786-5447
Delaware	Newark University of Delaware Library	(302) 451-2965
Dist. of	Washington: Howard University Libraries	(202) 636-5060
Columbia		
Florida	Fort Lauderdale: Broward County Main Library	(305) 357-7444
	Miami-Dade Public Library	(305) 375-2665
	Orlando University of Central Florida Libraries	(407) 275-2562
Georgia	Atlanta: Price Gilbert Memorial Library,	
	Georgia Institute of Technology	(404) 894-4508
Idaho	Moscow: University of Idaho Library	(208) 885-6235
Illinois	Chicago Public Library	(312) 269-2865
	Springfield: Illinois State Library	(217) 782-5430
Indiana	Indianapolis-Marion County Public Library	(317) 269-1741
Iowa	Des Moines: State Library of Iowa	(515) 281-4118
Kentucky	Louisville: Free Public Library	(502) 561-8617
Louisiana	Baton Rouge: Troy H. Middleton Library,	
	Louisiana State University	(504) 388-2570
Maryland	College Park: Engineering and Physical	
	Sciences Library, University of Maryland	(301) 454-3037
Massachusetts	Amherst: Physical Sciences Library,	
	University of Massachusetts	(413) 545-1370
	Boston Public Library	(617) 536-5400 Ext. 265
Michigan	Ann Arbor: Engineering Transportation	
	Library, University of Michigan	(313) 764-7494
	Detroit Public Library	(313) 833-1450
Minnesota	Minneapolis Public Library & Information Centre	(612) 372-6570
Missouri	Kansas City: Linda Hall Library	(816) 363-4600
	St Louis Public Library	(314) 241-2288 Ext. 376
Montana	Butte: Montana College of Mineral Science	
	and Technology Library	(406) 496-4281
Nebraska	University of Nebraska-Lincoln Library	(402) 472-3411
Nevada	Reno: University of Nevada Library	(702) 784-6579
New Hampshire	Durham: University Library	(603) 862-1777
New Jersey	Newark Public Library	(201) 733-7782
	Piscataway: Library of Science & Medicine,	
	Rutgers University	(201) 932-2895

New Mexico	Albuquerque: University of New Mexico Library	(505) 277-4412
New York	Albany: New York State Library	(518) 473-4636
	Buffalo and Erie County Public Library	(716) 858-7101
	New York Public Library (The Research Libraries)	(212) 714-8529
North Carolina	Raleigh: D H Hill Library, NC State University	(919) 737-3280
Ohio	Cincinnati & Hamiliton County, Public Library of	(513) 369-6936
	Cleveland Public Library	(216) 623-2870
	Columbus: Ohio State University Libraries	(614) 292-6175
	Toledo/Lucas County Public Library	(419) 259-5212
Oklahoma	Stillwater: Oklahoma State University Library	(405) 744-7086
Oregon	Salem: Oregon State Library	(503) 378-4239
Pennsylvania	Philadelphia: The Free Library	(215) 686-5331
	Pittsburgh: Carnegie Library of Pittsburgh	(412) 622-3138
	University Park: Pattee Library, Pennsylvania	
Rhode Island	Providence Public Library	(401) 455-8027
South Carolina	Charleston: Medical University of South Carolina Library	(803) 792-2371
Tennessee	Memphis & Shelby County Public Library and Information Center	(901) 725-8876
	Nashville: Vanderbilt University Library	(615) 322-2775
Texas	Austin: McKinney Engineering Library, University of Texas	(512) 471-1610
	College Station: Sterling C Evans Library, Texas A & M University	(409) 845-2551
	Dallas Public Library	(214) 670-1468
	Houston: The Fondren Library, Rice University	(713) 527-8101 Ext 2587
Utah	Salt Lake City: Marriott Library, University of Utah	(801) 581-8394
Virginia	Richmond: Virginia Commonwealth University Library	(804) 367-1104
Washington	Seattle: Engineering Library, University of Washington	(206) 543-0740
Wisconsin	Madison: Kurt F Wendt Engineering Library, University of Wisconsin	(608) 262-6845
	Milwaukee Public Library	(414) 278-3247

All of the above-listed libraries offer CASSIS (Classification And Search Support Information System), which provides direct, on-line access to Patent and Trademark Office data

mer German Democratic Republic, the Ilmenauer Institute of Technology specializes in patent documentation.

Uses of patent information

Collections of patents and files of patent data can be explored manually, or by means of the online techniques described in Chapter 9, in order to achieve three main objectives:

1.   To gain access to scientific and technical information
2.   To establish various aspects of the legal status of patents
3.   To obtain commercial intelligence

The first objective, gaining access to scientific and technical information, is the one to which most effort is devoted by searchers. It enables data to be gathered which both supplements and complements information in conventionally published sources, with an emphasis on early indications of new thinking, and detailed, albeit narrowly construed, descriptions of technical ideas. The approach provides access to information not usually published in any other form. Advantages often claimed by those responsible for the maintenance of such collections are that patents offer a form of 'free' technology, and provide an early warning system in key areas of development. The technique adopted will depend greatly on the nature of the subject area under scrutiny – searches in, for example, mechanical and electrical engineering will rely heavily on the opportunity to study circuits, diagrams and drawings, whereas the subject-matter searching of polymers and other chemical substances will demand skills in the use of fragmentation codes and ring index numbers. Such topics are discussed elsewhere in this book.

The second objective, to establish various aspects of the legal status of a patent, reflects the fact that industrial property is similar to any other form of property in that it can be bought, sold and bargained with. The main reasons such searches are conducted include validity, status and equivalence.

Validity searches are conducted to establish the technical strength of a patent. How, for example, would a patent fare if challenged in court? The means of assessing a patent's strength involve a knowledge and evaluation of the prior art cited against the patent during the substantive examination, and how the patentee overcame the cited prior art in his arguments to the examiner. In most countries the prior art cited in the prosecution of an application is listed in the published patent, or is available as an attached search report. More detailed information is available in the file of the prosecution of the application, and copies of the prosecution files of published patents are open to public inspection in a number of countries, including Great Britain, the United States and Germany. Similar provisions apply to the files of the European Patent Office.

Status searches are often conducted when relevant patents are found in the course of an infringement search, and seek to answer questions about formalities, most notably:

● Has an application proceeded to grant?

- Is a granted patent still in force?
- Has a patent been amended?
- Has a patent been assigned to someone else?
- Has a patent been licensed?
- Has a patent been endorsed 'licence of right'?

All patent authorities have rules[5] for the adminstration of such matters, and their non-observance can make a fundamental difference to the status of a patent. In Great Britain the publication *Reports ... of Patent Cases* (RPC) frequently contains details of problems which have arisen because renewal dates have been missed, or because fees which were due to be paid had not been paid. Although reminder systems are operated, the change in the status of patents can arise through default or oversight, in addition to deliberate lack of action by patentees who have decided not to continue paying renewal fees because of the rising scale of costs.

In Great Britain, a new page is opened in the statutory *Register of Patents* for each patent granted, giving details of the name of the patentee, the patent number and formalities information as appropriate. Registers are available for personal inspection and copies of extracts can be ordered by post.

The European Patent Office has a database which gives online information on the status of European applications, whilst INPADOC offers information on the legal status of documents published by 16 countries or organizations, with a response time which depends on the response time of the individual office concerned.

In the United States, the practice by which a patent, once granted, automatically remained in force left little need for status searches. However, an amendment introduced in 1981 provided for renewal fees as from 1986. They are set to recover a percentage of costs, and become due at 3.5, 7.5 and 11.5 years after publication. One result will be that in the course of time, the number of patents actually in force will decrease as owners decide it is no longer economic to maintain them.

Looking for equivalents to known patents is one of the most common reasons for online searching – the aim is often to determine the extent of protection already secured in other countries, although from an information point of view an equivalent specification may disclose an invention in a more accessible language. Access to patent families can be obtained by one of three routes: patent number, priority number or designated states.

The third major objective in seeking to exploit a collection of patents is to build up a fund of commercial intelligence by noting which companies are active in particular areas of technology. Some organizations seek to protect their investments in innovation by adopting a saturation technique, and patenting every single aspect of a particular development. The result is a portfolio of applications and granted patents which becomes an important bargaining counter when negotiating licensing agreements, and the length of the patents schedules can often influence the financial terms of a deal.

Good commercial intelligence depends as much on the quantitative as on the qualitative approach, and statistical analyses of patent information are made much more accessible through specially written programs, such as Derwent's PATSTAT Plus, which allows data to be downloaded to desktop computers for subjection to numerical analysis. Figures can be manipulated to establish trends by company, subject, time period, or whichever parameters are most appropriate. Information so derived can be used internally as a yardstick against which an organization can measure its strengths and weaknesses. Alternatively, it can be used in an external sense to chart the progress of an individual sector, and the relative performances of its major participants. Such studies reach across into areas of business not normally in day to day contact with patents material, especially market research departments and technology forecasting teams.

Exercises of this type are greatly facilitated when considering the United States, by two reports issued by the US Patent and Trademark Office. The first report[6] is a ranked listing of the 35 countries and more than 6000 organizations that received the most patents during the period 1969–1988. Yearly patent counts are shown for each country and organization. The second report[7] lists US and foreign organizations that received three or more US patents during the same period. It includes 28 000 corporations, government agencies and universities. For each organization, the report shows the total patent count for the 20 year period.

Finally, in contrast to all the positive attributes of patents when used as a source of information, it has to be pointed out that concern is growing that patent claims are becoming so wide that they have no meaning, and are a growing blight on patent information.[8] The problem has been identified as one in which too many claims are being allowed, which bear no relation to reality and are so broad that they cannot be indexed or retrieved. Part of the blame has been laid at the door of the European Patent

Table 8.2 Numbers of patents applied for in each major language

Year	English	German	Japanese	French	Other	Total
1989	9301	2399	1313	804	1057	14 874
1990	12 097	3098	1667	1071	1226	19 159

Office, which is allegedly anxious to relax the rules to make the EPO route more attractive to applicants. Clearly such serious imputations need detailed substantiation before any firm conclusions can be drawn.

Languages and translations

As in other forms of literature, the language in which an item is written greatly determines its availability and use. Patents are generally published in the official language of the country in which the issuing office is situated, an essential requirement if local enterprise is to be encouraged and nurtured. However, with the coming of the Patent Cooperation Treaty and the establishment of the European Patent Office, a number of changes have been introduced which help in some measure to overcome the language barrier.

In the case of the PCT, the administering office, WIPO, has two working languages, English and French, and the *PCT Gazette* is published in both. Many other WIPO publications appear in a variety of languages, including Arabic, Chinese, Dutch, German, Italian, Japanese, Portuguese, Russian and Spanish, whilst the languages most favoured by those submitting patent applications via the PCT route is English. Recent figures are found in Table 8.2.

In 1990, the language of filing for 39% of the 'Other' category was Swedish.

The European Patent Office has three official languages, English, French and German, and documents such as the annual report are arranged in three columns, one for each. Articles 67 and 65 of the European Patent Convention make provision, respectively, for the translation of the claims of an application and for the translation of the text of a specification, and contracting states may exercise a right to require translations in order to conform with their own national law. A synopsis of such regulations and requirements is contained in the brochure *National Law Relating to the EPC*.[9]

Further help is at hand from the American company Research Publications, which, in order to overcome the language barriers encountered by non-German or non-French speaking researchers, examiners or patent agents, makes available on an annual subscription basis a microfilm file called *EPO English Translations*. Each translation of a French or German language EPO patent is certified as accurate, and is prepared by a professional translator in accordance with the requirements of the British Patent Office. *EPO English Translations* are available from September 1987 onwards, and the collection now contains over 25 000 translations. The point about accuracy is particularly important, for a correct rendering is crucial for the proper interpretation of the text and claims, and the avoidance of costly disputes about meanings.

A further point on the issue of accuracy is that the very up-to-dateness of patents brings its own problems for translators asked to deal with texts needed for foreign filings. The American expression 'creeping fluid mass' (i.e. water to which a long-chain molecule slippery gel has been added) remains 'creeping fluid mass' in the text of German application DE 3920998.

Some words are not translated because everyone understands the worldwide usage, especially if backed by an international standard. Thus the ISO term 'sea container' is not rendered into German in DE 3922809. Hybrid terms can also be something of a problem; for instance the half-English, half-German term Wohnbox in DE 3924357 could possibly translate as 'living box' (on the analogy of Wohnzimmer, 'living room'), but 'living box' does not sound at all right in English, especially when the invention in question is temporary tent-like structure containing a sleeping berth, which can be erected over and fitted to the rear end of an ordinary passenger car. Wohnbox is undoubtedly succinct, but will it catch on?

Another term of recent origin is 'spoiler', which in the 1972 edition of *Chambers Twentieth Century Dictionary* was simply given as 'any thing or person that spoils', but which in the 1988 edition (retitled *Chambers English Dictionary*) had been expanded to 'an aerodynamic device fitted to the wings of an aircraft to reduce lift and assist descent; a similar device fitted to motor vehicles to lessen drag and reduce the tendency to become unstable through a lifting effect at high speeds'. In 1991 the word remained untranslated in DE 3930024, which concerned a loading platform for a car transporter designed to overcome problems associated with vehicles having spoilers, which because of their low ground clearance had been subject to damage when ascending the transporter ramp.

Problems of translation, and the high costs associated with the activity, are of major concern to inventors and applicants, who have little option but to incur the charges if their applications are to succeed in the countries of their choice.

As far as the patents information searcher is concerned, he is somewhat better placed than his colleagues handling the conventional literature. If a patent is identified as being of interest, but published in an unfamiliar language, a common strategy is to conduct a family search to see whether an equivalent specification has appeared in a more accessible language. Such a system works well, and is capable of identifying very quickly the required translations. Journal papers on the other hand are normally published once only, and searchers for the text in another language need to go through a coordinating agency such as the International Translations Centre.

References

1. Hill, M.W. (1988) Universal availability of patents, *Interlending and Document Supply*, **16**, (3), 89-94
2. Newton, D.C. (1990) from patchwork to network – patent information dissemination in the United Kingdom. *World Patent Information*, **12**, (1), 15-19
3. Hewish, J. (1980) *The indefatigable Mr Woodcroft – the legacy of invention*. London: British Library (History of Technology Series no 1)
4. *Guide to industrial property holdings* (1990) London: British Library, Science Reference and Information Service (SRIS)
5. *Patent Rules* (1990) London: HMSO (SI 1990/2384 replacing SI 1982/717)
6. Department of Commerce, Patent and Trademark Office (1989) *Industrial patent activity in the US: Part 1 Time series profile by company and country of origin, 1969-1988*. Springfield, Va: National Technical Information Service PB89-188650CAU
7. Department of Commerce, Patent and Trademark office (1989) Industrial patent activity in the US: Part 2 *Alphabetical listing by company, 1969-1988*. Springfield, Va: National Technical Information Service PB89-188668CAU
8. Patents: Norton warns (1990) *Information World Review*, September, p. 25
9. European Patent Office (1989) *National law relating to the EPC*, 6th edn. Munich: European Patent Office

CHAPTER NINE

Online searching techniques

J.M. SHAW

Searching techniques

The use of online searching has expanded rapidly since its introduction, and it is still a growth area; new databases are being added and continual improvements in the hosts' search systems are being made. Recently, big strides have been made in the use of CD-ROM as a means of information storage and retrieval.

In this chapter it is intended to cover techniques and strategies for online searching, pointing out pitfalls and giving guidelines which can be applied irrespective of which host or database is being used; and to give a brief outline of patent databases currently available.

Why online? In the United Kingdom and other countries there are very good libraries where patent literature can be consulted, both domestic and foreign. Subsidiary patent networks also exist, as for example the Patent Information Network (PIN). However, even for experienced searchers, there are problems. In the past it was quite often sufficient to carry out a search of one's own country's patents (in the UK it used to be only necessary to search the last 50 years). Now, with the alteration of patent law and the growth of multinational companies, an awareness of the international patent situation is required.

In order to carry out an international search manually it is necessary to have a working knowledge of at least a dozen languages. Although the domestic and international classifications will help shortlist the millions of patent documents kept in libraries, a manual search is still a time-consuming exercise. Online enables one to access the documentation quickly by subject (keyword and free text); bibliographic item (applicant, inventor, patent number, filing date, priority details, and so on); classification (domestic or IPC); or any combination of the above. Also available online is information about citations, references, patent families, equivalents and legal status. On some systems it is also possible to carry out statistical analysis. One can order copies of documents online, and have the results printed offline in either predesignated or user-defined formats.

On the debit side there are limits to how far back one can search (normally to the 1960s or 1970s, depending on the subject or file being used); the need to buy and set up equipment to carry out the searches; and the cost of online time and telecommunication charges, although these are to a large extent offset by the time saved.

Getting started

Two factors need to be considered initially:

1. Type of equipment
2. Which host(s) to sign up with

Choice of equipment depends on what is already available in-house – there are two main systems, a dumb terminal with printer, and a PC with slave printer and/or download facilities. It is not intended to enlarge on equipment choice, as most host companies can advise on this, and many large companies have systems analysts able to help as well.

Table 9.1 gives a list of the hosts and the patent files available on them. Points to consider when choosing a host are:

● Is there a signing-on fee?
● What other files on the host would be of interest?
● What subjects and countries are of special interest?

Talk to the host companies and, where possible, the file suppliers too, for quite often the same file appears on more than one host. Variations in the host's search system, depending on the subject normally searched, could favour one over another. It is quite an accepted policy to sign up with more than one host.

Carrying out an online search

Having signed up with host or hosts, attended a training session, read the training manual and become familiar with the login procedures, it is necessary to memorize the password. It should not be programmed into an automatic login system, because people have been known to use

Table 9.1 Hosts and patent files available on them

HOST	PATENT FILES
DIALOG	CLAIMS, CHINESE PATENTS, WPI/L INPADOC (legal status & family)
DATA-STAR	CPBM, CPEV
IRS-ESA	ITALPATS, SPACEPATENTS
ORBIT	APIPAT, CHINAPATS, CLAIMS, INPADOC, INPANEW, JAPIO, LEGSTAT, LITALERT, USPATENTS, USSTATUS, USCLASSIFICATION, WPI/L
QUESTEL	CIB, ECLATX, EDOC, EPAT, FPAT, JURINPI, PHARM, WPI/L
STN	APIPAT, CLAIMS, INPADOC, INPAMONITOR, PATDPA, PATGRAPH

someone else's password. The user is now ready to start searching, but first it is vital to preplan the strategy, for online time costs money. Once connected, both database and telecommunications charges are incurred.

One other general point needs emphasizing at the outset – be sure of what is being looked for. This may seem obvious, but whether carrying out a search for oneself or acting as an intermediary, it becomes apparent that different people call the same thing by different names, e.g. in the Midlands an off-licence is called an 'outdoor'! Other examples more relevant to patent searching are trade names (are they spelt correctly?) and chemical compounds (what different names are they known by?).

Patent searches tend to fall under one of the following headings, each of which is considered in turn, with the emphasis on preplanning the strategy. Firstly, subject searching: having made sure of what is being searched for, the first point to consider is the mode of search, which can be by classification, by keyword/free text, or by a combination of both. The second point is which files are to be searched, and the third the language of the database. Looking more closely at these aspects, in theory, classification should, if the subject matter has been correctly identified, give a perfect result. Unfortunately classification is open to differing interpretations, and IPC numbers can vary greatly, depending on the issuing office. Sometimes the subject in question does not fall neatly into a classification, and the searcher needs to rely on its being properly cross-classified; in addition, a general search may cut across several classes. Nevertheless, searching by classification can give very good results. Depending on the file being searched, there is a choice of classification systems: IPC; domestic (if searching a single country, as for example

CLAIMS, which covers US patents); or the file producer's own scheme (for example the Derwent classification). Moreover the user has the opportunity to produce his own tailor-made file, especially in INPADOC and USCLASSIFICATION.

Also under this heading comes the use of registry numbers for searching in the chemical and pharmaceutical areas, and the use of the Derwent fragment codes in the same fields. If cross-file searching is used, field qualifiers can be different – it is possible to redefine in ORBIT by means of the 'select' command, and such points should be checked in the hosts' manuals.

A useful technique to help to classify a subject is to carry out a 'dirty' search – that is, to put in a few broad, free-text terms in a file where such a procedure is possible, and to print out a few of the hits, (normally one would expect a lot of hits with this type of search) to see how they have been classified. Again, if the searcher knows of a patent in the right area, enter it in say WPI/L, as the Derwent record contains all the IPC numbers allocated to the complete family, which can be fruitful and illuminating. Finally it should be remembered that class marks can be combined by the use of 'and' and 'or', where 'and' means both terms must appear, whilst 'or' means either or both terms.

Keyword and/or free-text searching can be as simple or as sophisticated as required. One can put in a few broad terms to retrieve hits in the right area, and probably a lot in the wrong area too! Word searching can, if carried out properly, be a very important means of subject searching. In this area, search techniques such as Boolean logic, truncation, proximity searching, use of brackets, and so on, come into their own. However this area also has its pitfalls.

The above points will now be illustrated by means of examples. If one has been asked for information on 'Moulds', the first question is, what type? – jelly moulds, sandcasting moulds, diecasting dies, or what? As stated earlier, be sure of what is being asked for; if necessary go back to the original enquirer. The true subject turns out to be sandcasting moulding machines with the mould sand packed by centrifugal force. With this much clearer picture, one can start to formulate a search strategy such as:

S moulding and machines	-s1
S s1 and packing	-s2
S s2 and centrifugal	-s3

This is a simple strategy which will produce results, but it needs more consideration. The first thing is the spelling of 'Mould', which is English and not the American 'Mold'. In order to cross-file search both English and American produced files, it becomes necessary to truncate internally. In addition the subject could be indexed under 'Mould' or 'Moulds', requiring a further truncation. The same applies to 'Machine' and 'Machines'. Thus the first search statement would be modified as:

S mo#ld: and machine:

(NB: symbols used in these illustrations are those employed on ORBIT). Again, one would have to truncate 'packing' and 'centrifugal', and assuming at this stage there were no synonyms, the final search statement would be:

S mo#ld: and machine:	-s1
S sl and pack:	-s2
S s2 and centrifugal:	-s3

By using brackets, the search statement could be entered as S(mo#ld: and machine:) and (pack: and centrifugal:) S1. However brackets should be treated with care, as it is useful to get an idea of the postings step by step, especially if one of the terms used is too restrictive. The above search illustrates the use of truncation and spelling variations, but another point to watch for is a difference in meaning between English and American words, for instance, 'pants' (US) equals 'trousers' (UK).

When using truncation it is necessary to consider how many terms the truncation will produce. If, in the above example, the word 'sand' had been truncated, the following terms would have been searched: sand, sands, sanded, sanding, sander, sandbank, sandbag, and so on. In other words, all the terms in the database starting with 'sand'. It may therefore be advisable on occasion to enter the required terms individually, plus 'or'. Still on the subject of truncation and term selection, the use of the 'neighbour' or 'expand' commands to browse the files index can be very profitable.

The next example shows how the same subject can be described in various ways. If a request for a search on ABS systems comes from a client in the motor industry, it can be taken that he means antiskid braking systems, which immediately gives two terms. Are there others? On questioning the client it will emerge that the following terms are also relevant: antilock, antiblock, wheel spin and wheel spin detection/sensing. By neighbouring/expanding the term 'antiskid', the following results are achieved:

Term	Comments
anti-skid	with hyphen
anti skid	two words
antiskid	one word
anti-skidding	with hyphen and -ing
anti skidding	two words and -ing
antiskidding	one word and -ing

The same variations appear for both antilock and antiblock, and there can also be skid sensing or skid detecting or sensing skidding or detecting skidding.

For 'wheel spin' the variations are:

● detect wheel spin

● detection of wheel spin

● wheel spin detection

● onset of wheel spin

● sensing of wheel spin

Having sorted out the various possible forms, how are they put into a coherent search strategy? Basically by the use of truncation and proximity searching, where proximity searching is the technique of searching either for adjacent words in the text, or for words within a certain distance of each other, or in the same sentence or field. In the illustration, ORBIT terms are used again.

(w) or ( ) retrieves terms adjacent each other in the order specified
(wn) retrieves terms more than n terms apart in the order specified (n=1-255)
(s) retrieves in the same sentence in any order
(f) retrieves terms in the same field

The search strategy develops thus:

S antiskid: or anti (w2) skid: -s1

Note that antiskid: covers antiskid and antiskidding, whilst anti(w2)skid: covers anti-skid, anti-skidding, anti skid and anti skidding.

S antiblock: or anti(w2)block: -s2
S antilock: or anti(w2)lock: -s3

Alternatively, brackets could be used and the search entered:

(antiskid: or anti(w2)skid:) or (antiblock: or anti(w2)block:)
or (antilock: or anti(w2)lock:)   -s1

Looking now at the 'wheel spin' variations, there are two terms – 'sense' and 'detect' – which if entered in a truncated form can cause problems, because both are very highly posted and could create computer time overflow problems. Such terms need to be treated with caution, and if they can be omitted, do so. Possible solutions are:

1.   Enter wheel(w2)spin, or possibly 'wheel' and 'spin' to see what

the postings are, and then decide whether to qualify with 'sense' or 'detect'.

2. Combine the broad IPC (B60T) for brakes with 'and' spin

3. If searching WPI/L, combine the broad Derwent class for brakes Q18.

If looking for systems, (2) and (3) would be good, but if looking for hardware, items such as sensors, which are classified only under H02k, could be missed.

Yet another example of what appears to be a simple search concerns 'Sialon', a ceramic consisting of silicon, aluminium, oxygen and nitrogen. Should it be entered as sialon; silicon oxynitride; aluminium, silicon and nitrogen; or under the appropriate chemical symbols? Here the use of the chemical coding systems developed by the database producers and hosts will be of great value. If, however, the search is for applications and means of making articles in sialon, this would entail cutting across classes, and keywords and free-text searching come into their own.

In the above examples, the use of field qualifiers has not been mentioned, but for searches by classification the appropriate qualifier would have to be used. With word searching, most host systems default to the basic index, and a field qualifier is only needed when searching the title or using index terms.

False drops, that is, retrieving hits which are in a different subject field, must be expected. The entry of the terms 'anti-bounce' and 'contact' in a search relating to electrical contacts, retrieved details of an athletic brassière! False drops are inevitable, and the searcher must not be afraid of casting the net too wide. An assessment of the material can always be carried out afterwards and irrelevant items discarded.

Name searching is an area many people think is easy, but there are a number of problems, not least the question of correct spelling, and here it is appropriate to introduce a personal note: there are at least two patents to my name with my name as an inventor; let us assume you have had a telephone request to find them. The first thing to consider is how is the name spelt – Shaw or Shore? Secondly, what are my forenames? I have been called by my second name, Malcolm, since I was 5, and the request probably asked for Malcolm Shaw's patents. Many people are not aware of my first name, so how would one go about looking for the patents in question? They could be in the database under:

M ? Shaw
? M Shaw
M Shaw
M ? Shore

? M Shore
M Shore

Shaw is a fairly common name, and clearly more information is needed. The only further piece of information is that I worked for Lucas Industries. This is in fact a vital clue, and will enable the search to be carried out successfully. First of all, enter:

S(Shaw/in or Shore/in) and Lucas/pa.

This should give a hit from which you will learn that the correct name is J.M. Shaw. Go back into the database and neighbour/expand Shaw J/in to cover the other possibilities, such that I may have worked for someone else, or that my forenames may have been entered in full and not just as initials. My new name in the file could be:

Shaw J
Shaw J M
Shaw John M
Shaw John Malcolm
Shaw J Malcolm

The above points are equally valid when looking for patents filed in the United States, where applications have to be filed in the inventor's name and then assigned to the company for which the inventor works. This means that US files such as CLAIMS and US PATENTS are very good for searching by inventor. Of the two major general files, INPADOC and WPI/L, INPADOC lists all inventors if named on the original document. Treat Derwent WPI/L files with more caution, although they are also very good for patents in individuals' names.

As regards searches for patents by corporate names, most of what has been noted above is valid, especially with verbal requests and spelling variants. Other areas which can cause problems are trade names, companies generally known by initials, and subsidiary companies.

Many companies are known by their trade names but actually file under their registered names. A good example is Hella, a German firm in the automotive field. Searching the files under Hella would at one time have yielded no hits, but by checking in a trademark database, it would have become evident that the correct name was Westfälische Metall Industrie KG Hueck & Co. Nowadays the firm does file under Hella KG Hueck & Co. See, for example, GB 1492950 Pneumatic control of headlamps, and GB 2211007 Electrical circuit arrangement.

The next thing to look for is initials. A lot of companies are known just by their initials, for example, GEC, ICI and FEMSA. In consequence, one has to establish how the name is entered in the database (ICI or Imperial Chemical Industries?). If a quick search of the patent assignee index by means of the neighbour/ expand commands establishes that the company does in fact file under its full name (i.e. no postings under the initials) how does one determine what the full name is? Experience here can help by knowing what the initials usually stand for (e.g. G = General, F = Fabbrica, etc). Other good measures are references to trade literature, and of course a query to the client to see if he knows. Derwent, in their WPI/L files, use a company code and used to publish a coding manual which proved invaluable. The other point to watch for is companies with the same, or very similar, initials, of which the classic example is GE (General Electric Company of America) and GEC (General Electric Company plc of Great Britain).

There is one additional point to look out for – abbreviations. Database producers abbreviate a lot of commonly occurring words, such as gen for general, univ for university, and so forth. They do, however, have lists of the standard abbreviations they use.

We have considered companies with variant names, but it is also necessary to address public bodies, learned institutions and similar corporate concerns. These can quite often be under a different name from the one expected. For example, government-funded work in the UK is quite often in the name of the department actually spending the money, as for instance Ministry of Defence. With universities, sometimes the patents are filed in the university's name, sometimes in the name of the person carrying out the work, sometimes in the name of whoever funded the work. Research institutions may be known by their full name, or often by initials or an acronym (e.g. MIRA – Motor Industry Research Association). It is also necessary to watch for subsidiary companies, which may choose to file under the subsidiary name or under the name of the parent firm, with a few filing under both. In such cases, directories such as *Who owns whom* are invaluable.

One final pitfall to note is when original patents have been assigned to another company. What happens here is that the client is aware of a company making a particular product, and wants details of any patents. If on searching a blank is drawn, there are three possible reasons:

1. There are no filings.

2. They have not yet been published (a possibility in the United States, but not in countries with early publication).

3. The patents are in someone else's name and have either been assigned or licensed to the company known to be making the product.

Unfortunately there is no easy solution to this problem. It can sometimes be resolved by a subject search, or by a search of the literature or press databases. A good example is the case of a request for patents on means for detecting obstacles behind a vehicle. The clue given was a company's name and the fact that the idea had been described in the press. The name search drew a blank, but a look in the press database located an article which revealed the inventors' names and the fact that the patent had been assigned to the company whose name had been mentioned originally.

Patent families/equivalents

Provided one has been given the correct information and the patents in the family have been filed 'in convention', there should not be too many problems. However, there are a few things to watch out for which can influence the choice of database and the method of searching. The first is the choice of database, and this will depend on what is being looked for, i.e. the complete family, just certain countries (which may be the ones the requesting client manufactures in), or a single-language equivalent, e.g. an English-language equivalent to a Japanese patent. INPADOC will give the most complete answer, but it is the most expensive; EDOC covers 17 major countries including Japan, and costs less than INPADOC. WPI/L covers 30 major patent-issuing countries, but its Japanese coverage is not complete, especially in the older electrical and mechanical fields. It is, however, good for sorting out divisionals, continuations in part, and multiple priorities, as these are cross-referenced. Derwent also try to match up 'out of convention' filings where these are obvious. Files such as CLAIMS, FPAT and PATDPA, i.e. single-country files, are useful when looking for an equivalent in the particular countries they cover.

Next, it is necessary to establish whether the number provided by the client is a patent application, publication or laid open to inspection number, a fact not always obvious, especially with Japanese items. Which number it turns out to be will affect the field qualifier used.

Be on the lookout for divisionals, continuations in part and multiple priorities – quite often it is necessary to enter all priorities and/or patent numbers to get the complete picture. As noted above, Derwent, in their WPI/L files are good at cross-referencing patent families.

Finally out-of-convention filings: these quite often occur if the filings are in the name of a small company or an individual. They are not quite so common now, as most major countries publish early, but occur among older patents and those originating in the United States, which of course do not have early publication. Most large companies fortunately do tend to file in convention, and if an out-of-convention filing is suspected, one has to carry out a search in the individual's or company's name in the appropriate subject and time-span, and then make an assessment.

To summarize the above:

1. Establish whether it is a complete family, partial family, or just a single-language equivalent that is required.
2. Make sure to what document type the number provided actually refers.
3. Watch out for divisionals, continuations in part, multiple priorities and so on.
4. Make sure of the cost and coverage of the files to be used.
5. If necessary use more than one file, especially when it is important to obtain the whole family.

Status and citations

Certain files now carry legal status information and details of oppositions. INPADOC has the largest coverage as far as legal status data is concerned, although not all patent offices supply INPADOC with the relevant information. It is best to familiarize oneself with which countries are covered, by consulting INPADOC's literature and updating sheets. Files covering a single issuing body's or country's patents, such as EPAT, FPAT and PTTDPA which cover EPs & PCTs, French and German patents respectively, deal with both legal status and oppositions. This is an expanding field and it is worthwhile keeping a watch on the database producers' updates.

Databases such as CLAIMS, EPAT, FPAT, PATDPA and US PATENTS carry a citation field which is printable, and in some cases searchable. This is the case in CLAIMS CITATION on DIALOG and US PATENTS on ORBIT, where one can search to see what patents and literature references have been cited against a particular patent. This ability to find out what has been cited against a patent, by means of online searching, is of special benefit to the information searcher, as it can help to build up quite quickly a picture of what patents there are in a given subject area (one is using the examiner's expertise here), and the results can complement one's own search efforts.

Useful online options

Although this chapter is not intended as a training manual, there are certain online commands and options which are worth highlighting. They are:

SDI – SDI stands for Selective Dissemination of Information, a command used to initiate the automatic current-awareness service for a stored search in a user-specified database. Offline prints are automatically issued when the base is updated.

Electronic offline printing – most major hosts now offer this service as a means of obtaining prints online by requesting them to be printed in a special base with a low online charge. Normally there is a 2 hour delay before printing them, but nevertheless this is a great timesaver over offline prints.

Help/Explain – most hosts provide the means to obtain information about their services, a useful facility for infrequently used files.

On Tap/Training files – such files carry part of the information that appears in the main file; they are charged at a low rate and are intended to be used for self-training. However, they are useful if one is going to employ a complex search strategy, since this can be entered in a training file and then run as a 'saved search' in the main file.

Cost – most files have a means of keeping track of charges incurred when carrying out a search, a feature especially useful for recharging purposes.

Interrupting the search – commands such as 'break' and 'escape', which vary with the host in use, enable the searcher to stop the computer carrying out the function it has been instructed to do; an important feature if an error has been spotted

Save – one can normally save, either temporarily or permanently, another important facility well worth becoming familiar with.

Offline prints – these are are a cost-saving option when an enquiry is not urgent.

Downloading – a means of capturing data with suitable software on a PC and then editing it into a format appropriate to the client's needs.

Statistical analysis – two systems are available, Derwent's PATSTAT, which facilitates the analysis of downloaded material for use in graphs and charts, and the GET command on ORBIT, which permits a less elaborate but still satisfactory analysis.

Patent databases available for online searching

Patent databases basically fall into one or more of the following categories:

1. Those containing information about several countries' patents
2. Those containing information about a single country's patents

3. Those containing information about one subject
4. Those concerned with legal status, litigation and classification

Table 9.1 lists hosts and the files they carry, whilst Table 9.2 indicates files by host. Table 9.3 summarizes categories (1) to (4) above, probably the most important of which is category (1), containing three broad databases, namely EDOC, INPADOC and WPI/L.

Table 9.2 Patent files by individual hosts

PATENT FILE/S	HOST/S
APIPAT	ORBIT, STN
CLAIMS	DIALOG, ORBIT, STN
CHINAPATS	ORBIT
CHINESE PATENTS	DIALOG
CIB	QUESTEL
CPBM, CPEV	DAT-STAR
ECLATX	QUESTEL
EDOC	QUESTEL
EPAT	QUESTEL
FPAT	QUESTEL
INPADOC	DIALOG, ORBIT, STN
INPANEW	ORBIT
INPAMONITOR	STN
ITAL PAT	IRS-ESA
JAPIO	ORBIT
JURNIPI	QUESTEL
LEGSTAT	ORBIT
PATDPA	STN
PATGRAPH	STN
PHARM	QUESTEL
SPACEPATENTS	IRS-ESA
US PATENTS	ORBIT
US CLASSIFICATION	ORBIT
WPI/L	DIALOG, ORBIT, QUESTEL

Table 9.3 Summary of file catgories and patent files available

FILE CATEGORY	PATENT FILE/S
MULTICOUNTRY, MULTI-SUBJECT COVERAGE	EDOC, INPANEW, INPAMONITOR, WPI/L.
SINGLE COUNTRY, MULTI-SUBJECT COVERAGE	CHINAPATS, CHINESE PATENTS, CLAIMS, EPAT, FPAT, ITALPAT JAPIO, PATDPA, PATGRAPH, US PATENTS.
SUBJECT COVERAGE	APIPAT, CAS, CPBM, CPEV, PHARM, SPACEPATENTS.
LEGAL STATUS, CLASSIFICATION, OPPOSITIONS	CIB, ECLATX, EPAT, FPAT INPADOC, INPAMONITOR, JURNIPI, LEGSTAT, PATDPA, US CLASSIFICATION.

EDOC is produced by the Institut de la Propriété Industrielle (INPI) and is available on Questel. It contains information on patents and applications from 17 major industrialized countries, as well as European and PCT documents, plus those issued by the Organisation Africaine de la Propriété Intellectuelle (ORPI). EDOC is searchable by patent number, application number, priority details and the European and Dutch classifications; best used in conjunction with ECLATX, the European Classification file.

INPADOC, INPANEW, INPAMONITOR and LEGSTAT are produced by the International Patent Documentation Centre (INPADOC), and are available either directly from Vienna or on DIALOG, ORBIT and STN. They are loaded as one file on DIALOG, which includes both family and legal status data; as three files on ORBIT (INPADOC, INPANEW and LEGSTAT, with INPANEW containing the most recent 6-weeks' data); and as two files on STN, called INPADOC AND INPAMONITOR, which again covers the most recent information.

INPADOC, the organization of which is described in Chapter 7, is basically a bibliographic file with extensive legal status coverage (see (4) below). INPADOC is very good for searching by IPC patentee and inventor, and in addition is the only file that lists UK applications before publication (the same information as found in the *Official Journal (Patents)*). The database is excellent for patent families, with good coverage, but is expensive.

WPI/L (World Patent Index/Latest) is produced by Derwent Publications and is available on DIALOG, ORBIT and QUESTEL. Details of the Derwent range of activities are provided in Chapter 7. All members of a patent family are incorporated as one single record, and each record is comprehensively indexed and searchable by free text, IPC, and the Derwent classification. In addition, chemical and pharamaceutical patents are searchable by special Derwent codes. Chemical formulae are searchable on Questel by means of Questel's DARC, or the Markush DARC system. There is restricted access to certain parts of the file for non-Derwent subscribers, and also a two-level charging system, with Derwent subscribers having preferential rates. This file is a must for all patent searchers.

Files covering individual countries (category (2)) include the following:

CHINAPATS – produced by the Patent Documentation Service Center of the Patent Office of the People's Republic of China, and provided by INPADOC; available on ORBIT.

CHINESE PATENT ABSTRACTS IN ENGLISH – again produced by the Patent Documentation Service Center and provided by INPADOC; available on DIALOG.

CLAIMS – produced by IFI Plenum Corporation and available and DIA-LOG, ORBIT and STN; CLAIMS is an important series covering aspects of information on US patents back to 1950.

EPAT – produced by INPI and available on Questel; a file which covers all European patents and applications registered since 1968.

FPAT – produced by INPI and available on Questel; a register of French patents since 1969.

ITALPAT – produced by the Informacijski Centre, Ljubljana, and available on ESA/IRS; coverage for Italian patents since the early 1980s.

JAPIO – produced by the Japanese Patent Information Organization and available on ORBIT; coverage from 1966.

PATDPA, PATGRAPH – Produced by the Deutsches Patentamt in conjunction with the Fachinformationszentrum (FIZ); all German patents since 1968 are covered, with PATGRAPH acting as a subfile for the graphical searching of drawings, chemical structures and mathematical formulae; available on STN.

US PATENTS – produced by Derwent and available on ORBIT; gives front-page information on US patents published since 1971.

Files primarily concerned with subject (category (3)) include:

APIPAT – produced by the American Petroleum Institute and available on ORBIT and STN; covers the petroleum industry in selected countries from 1964 (worldwide from 1982).

CAS – produced by *Chemical Abstracts* and available under various file names on a number of hosts; not primarily a patent base, but far too important a file in chemistry not to be included here.

CPBM – produced by Current Patents Ltd and available on DATA-STAR; an expanding coverage of pharmaceutical patents.

CPEV – produced by Current Patents Ltd and also available on DATA-STAR; deals with the evaluation of pharmaceutical patents.

PHARM – produced by INPI and available on Questel; covers European, French and US pharmaceutical patents, with extended coverage planned back to 1961.

SPACEPATENTS – produced by ESA/HQ and available on ESA/IRS; covers the period 1984–1990, but is no longer updated.

Finally, files dealing with legal status, litigation and classification (category (4)) include the following;

CIB – produced by INPI and available on Questel; French version of the IPC.

ECLATX – produced by INPI and available on Questel; contains the full-text of the European Patent Classification Scheme.

LEGSTAT – Legal Status, produced by INPADOC and available on DIALOG, ORBIT and STN; comprehensive legal status information from many offices.

JURINPI – produced by INPI and available on Questel; details of French and European patents subject to legal attack.

LitAlert – produced by Rapid Patent Service Research Publications-and available on ORBIT; gives details of infringement actions in the United States.

PATENT STATUS FILE – produced by Rapid Patent Service Research Publications and available on ORBIT commencing 1991; intended as a comprehensive coverage of status issues in the United States.

US CLASSIFICATION – produced by Derwent and available on ORBIT; comprehensive file on all US classification issues since 1790.

Hosts and gateways

From the above it will be seen that the most important patent databases are available on DIALOG, ORBIT, QUESTEL and STN, with two specialist bases on DATA-STAR and two minor files on IRS-ESA. The selection of a host depends largely on what areas are of interest, and what other files on the host are also of use. The main hosts provide what they term a cluster of files, to give an all-round patent searching capability – the emphasis of the cluster varies from host to host, and selection is mainly a matter of personal choice.

Gateways are a relatively recent development, acting as intermediaries between a user and a database. A request is put to a gateway organization which then translates it into the commands necessary to search a range of databases, without the user needing to know about the retrieval language. Another feature is that a gateway can be accessed in the user's language and not that of the database. At present there are no gateways specifically for patents searching, but the whole field of databases, hosts and gateways has been surveyed in a companion volume in this series, namely *Online searching – principles and practice.*[1] Another useful title is *Online searching in science and technology*, from the British Library.[2] For news of new databases the user can consult the *Directory of Online Databases*,[3] published twice a year with quarterly updates; in 1990 the *Directory* listed over 70 databases under the heading 'patents'.

References

1. Hartley R.J. *et al.*, (1989) *Online searching – principles and practice*. London: Bowker-Saur
2. *Online searching in science and technology* (1990) London: British Library, Science Reference and Information Service (SRIS)
3 *Directory of online databases*, vol 11 (1990). New York: Cuadra/Elsevier

CHAPTER TEN

Information needs in the engineering industries

Introduction

In considering the patents literature as a source of information for engineers, it is as well to recall that various studies and surveys over the years have shown that, compared with their colleagues in physics and chemistry, practising engineers, especially those working in industry, are not particularly information conscious. That is to say, on the one hand they write a great deal less about their work compared with professionals in other disciplines, and on the other hand they tend to use bibliographically organized resources such as abstracts and indexes as sources to turn to only when all other avenues have been exhausted. If asked what action they take when in need of information, engineers will typically reply with a list that places great priority on personal contacts with fellow engineers, ready access to office files and reports, and the availability of trade journals and conference summaries. The same list will place minimum priority on libraries and information centres, despite the organized resources offered themselves or provided access to in the form of collections, indexes and abstracts.

Many engineers' desks, and nearly all engineering offices, will find some space for key textbooks, major reference handbooks, compilations of standards specifications, and the current issues of a range of relevant periodicals and learned journals. Such items of literature are just part of the vast array of information sources available to engineers, and the whole field is comprehensively described in *Information sources in engineering*.[1]

What is less frequently seen is evidence of patents literature, a state of affairs explained partly by the inherent difficulty of the material and partly by the fact that the few engineers who have a genuine affinity for the genre tend to act as gatekeepers on behalf of their fellow workers, who, recognizing the specialist nature of patents, are only too happy to leave the study of their contents to those who understand them. In theory, of course, all engineers use patents literature as a source of information, but in practice most use is made by a small proportion of enthusiastic specialists. The emphasis does change somewhat when an individual engineer becomes an inventor himself, or when he becomes closely involved in defending an alleged infringement.

Engineers as direct users

Of all the various categories of engineers who do make a specialization of patents as a source of information, there are two types in particular which merit further discussion, namely individual inventors and engineers working in teams or on projects concerned with research, development and design.

Individual inventors, also known as private inventors, are usually engineers, sometimes qualified, sometimes by dint of experience, who work alone with limited resources; they are members of a dwindling but persistent band of entrepreneurs attempting to match their ingenuity with the extensive facilities and back-up resources of large organizations. Such inventors are characterized by a dogged optimism, and have special needs with regard to information about the state of the prior art in their chosen field, because in pursuing and promoting their ideas they must be as certain as is reasonably possible that their inventions have not been anticipated or exploited elsewhere. Most large engineering companies receive a steady stream of ideas from outside inventors, usually offering improvements to existing products but sometimes suggesting a completely new concept. In many cases, such inventors are disappointed because they find their ideas have already been considered and discarded, not once but many times, and often on commercial rather than technical grounds.

Individual inventors in the field of engineering, sometimes unkindly referred to by patent agents as 'gadgeteers', often take a lot of time and trouble to explain their ideas, with detailed descriptions and meticulous drawings; other inventors prefer a vague approach and provide the sketchiest of outlines. In both cases, however, the need for information on what has been done before is vital.

The person with just one idea, maybe amounting to the pejorative *idée fixe*, inspired perhaps by a frustrating experience with a car which will not start in frosty weather, or alarmed by the problems of judging the relative speeds of vehicles on motorways, needs early and impartial advice. As a first step, before incurring any expense, he can attend a patents clinic of the type described in Chapter 4; alternatively, he can approach bodies such as the Automobile Association, which in 1990 announced a scheme whereby members of the public can submit technical ideas for preliminary examination.

The direct approach to a large company is, in fact, a well-tried route much favoured by the individual inventor. However, as noted in a widely reviewed study by Bain and Co.,[2] one of the most common complaints made about large companies by small innovators is the difficulty of finding the right person to contact to assess their invention. Many companies do not have a designated department or individual to assess external ideas. Even in companies with an identifiable contact point there is often a clear bias against external innovation. Some companies believe that, by admitting that there may be a role for a new product of process from outside, they are suggesting that their own R&D department is not doing its job properly.

On the other hand, there is plenty of evidence to show that formally opening the doors to outside innovation can result in a succession of letters, phone calls and even visits from persistent and sometimes misguided inventors, rather than a stream of interesting ideas worthy of proper (and of course time-consuming) technical evaluation.

In contrast, the person with a permanent inventive streak who produces one idea after another has a different set of problems, and one way of overcoming them is to join a body of fellow enthusiasts such as the Institute of Patentees and Inventors, an organization which acts as a coordinating body to encourage and promote individual inventors. The Institute also publishes a journal, *Future and the Inventor*, and a bulletin, *New Patents*, to bring innovations to the notice of manufacturers.

Engineers working in teams are fortunate in comparison with their solitary colleagues, in that they have the security of employment and the reassurance of adequate resources available to support the follow-up of promising ideas. If a team engineer comes up with a new development he can, in contrast to the lone inventor, request, as a matter of routine, a prior-art search of whatever comprehensiveness he feels appropriate, in order to see what are the likely chances of success for the invention. Team engineers can have access to many of the abstracting and indexing services discussed elsewhere in this book, although, as noted above, not many engineers are enthusiastic about studying abstracts on a routine basis. For those that do, the information yield can be considerable, and a properly constructed search strategy conducted in cooperation with information specialists can provide data in the following areas:

● *Patentability* – since all patent publications are part of the prior art, information contained in them is relevant to the question of whether or not a later invention is new or non-obvious.

● *Latest thinking* – as patents disclose information before conventional journals, they constitute a specialized indicator of the state of the art.

● *Competitors' activities* – current-awareness profiles can be tailored to monitor the patenting activities of competitors by noting applicants rather than subjects.

Scope of the ideas revealed

If an engineer decides to use patents as a source of information, either by studying the files himself or by asking an intermediary such as an information specialist to do so, what exactly can he expect to find? The general points about patentability, the state of the art and competitors' activities have already been noted. The consideration still to be determined is the nature and quality of the information gleaned from a detailed review of the patents relevant to a particular field of enquiry.

Two main points need to be emphasized. Firstly, patents are legal documents, the purpose of which is to define a legal right. In consequence, the style of presentation differs markedly from that of a paper in a journal, which can afford to be discursive where appropriate and discuss examples when necessary. Patents must, of course, have a legally sufficient description of the inventions which they claim, and the information so disclosed is generally more recent than that available in papers and similar published sources, which often have delaying mechanisms such as referees and review bodies anxious to impose standards of excellence and consistency. On the other hand, patents are normally applied for in the early stages of a project, at the time when an inventor has not yet sorted out all his ideas yet is under pressure to establish his priority rights to try and ensure an eventual commercial advantage.

Secondly, patents in engineering reveal, in the main, gradual developments, small advances, and modest improvements. Rarely are major breakthroughs or significant discoveries disclosed, although it is true that from time to time ideas catch the imagination of the technical press and indeed the general press, and considerable publicity ensues for the inventors and applicants. Two recent examples of this kind of exposure are reports of Captain Heinz Lipschutz's flying submarine[3], a vessel described as a U-plane which operates like an underwater aircraft; and Michael Passmore's planar system based on interlocking triangles,[4] which potentially has application in the design of oil rigs, aircraft wings, earthquake-proof houses, space stations and ships.

Sadly, attempts to register early filings may also be regarded as an 'unseemly rush', as was widely noted in the controversy over the announcements that cold fusion had successfully been achieved in a test tube.[5]

A large number of inventions represent new solutions to old problems, as exemplified by the famous quotation attributed to Emerson: 'If a man can make a better mouse-trap than his neighbour, though he build his house in the woods, the world will make a beaten path to his door'. Engineers and scientists work on a gradualist basis, if not in a quest for perfection, at least for a goal of refinement and optimization.

A good example is provided by the automobile industry, which now has 100 years' history manifested in scores of major developments, and many thousands of minor, cumulative changes. The big developments can best be appreciated by a visit to a major automotive museum such as the one in Turin, Italy, where an international collection of vehicles, admirably displayed and technically documented, vividly demonstrates the transition from horseless carriage to modern motor car.

The gradual, almost imperceptible changes, however, are most closely chronicled in patents, which still continue to issue in large numbers from large corporations and lone inventors alike. Activity is divided between tackling basic problems as old as the car itself, and with sorting out new ones brought about, for example, by the requirements of legislation.

Thus a survey of current patents in the automotive field will reveal applications relating to fundamental aspects of vehicle design and performance such as brakes, cooling, gears, lubrication, seals, steering, suspensions, valves and windows; and to aspects determined by public concern for safety and the environment, including air bags, catalytic converters, engine management systems, seat belts and snow chains.

A further group of automotive patents is concerned with what may be termed optional embellishments, and encompasses such items as bicycle carriers, interior trim, sunroofs and towing brackets. A great deal of engineering effort also goes into engines themselves, where individual inventors are particularly well represented in an endless search for a design which is a real and workable alternative to the reciprocating engine with its many moving parts.

Inventions in the automotive field can be non-specific (i.e. confined to no particular type of vehicle), or they can be concerned exclusively with particular types. Current applications for patents include both the broad categories such as cars, coaches and vans, and the highly specialized forms of transport such as lorries for carrying large sheets of glass.

As noted above, the automobile sector has been considered by way of example; a similar appraisal of any other major engineering field would undoubtedly disclose similar characteristics and principles. Whatever the field, once a body of patents has been identified (not always as easy as it might seem, when faced with applicants' expressions such as 'vehicles, especially ships'), the next question a searcher needs to address is, what are the claimed advantages of the ideas uncovered?

Once again, a pattern emerges which tends to confirm the gradualist nature of patents, for a study of the particular section in each specification which talks about the aim of the invention will yield a list which is valid for almost any branch of engineering. Reasons typically given in support of an invention include:

- To reduce noise
- To save space
- To reduce manufacturing costs
- To improve performance
- To reduce weight
- To save material
- To replace material, e.g. ceramic for metal
- To facilitate maintenance
- To prevent undue-wear
- To extend operating life
- To reduce the number of components

In examining the scope of the information revealed in engineering patents, the point needs to be made that most of the specifications relate to products rather than processes. The reason engineers usually advance for this state of affairs is that process patents are difficult to police. Whereas products can be placed side by side for comparison, and if necessary, taken apart using reverse engineering techniques in order to try and see just where the novelty lies, the secrets associated with processes are not so easily discovered.

Methods to improve the surface properties of metals, for example, can range from case hardening to ion implantation, but the practical difficulties in determining which route was taken to achieve a particular effect are enormous. Thus if an inventor reveals his method, there is a very real danger that it may be copied by competitors without fear of detection. By deciding not to disclose a process, an inventor can prevent others from using it, and at the same time save the expense of patent cover.

Limitations

Information gleaned from patents is not without its limitations, especially if it is to be put to practical use by relating it to and integrating it with existing information from other sources to build up a broader picture. Several aspects make its application difficult. Firstly there is the simple issue of the titles of patents – some can be explicit, even wordy, such as 'Arrangement for the catalytic cleaning or similar of combustion engine exhaust gases with two exhaust gas treatment bodies and a protective ring in between' (EP 0387422); others can be unbelievably curt, such as 'Seat' (DE 3908777), which actually refers to a car seat with an adjustable support for the lumbar region. It may also be noted that the length of a patent application can vary from a couple of hundred words (including claims) to several hundred pages.

Then there is the question of the quality of drawings and diagrams, since the usefulness of patents covering engineering inventions is greatly enhanced by the presence of figures, and indeed it is essential to read the text in conjunction with them. Regrettably the standard of draughtsmanship varies a great deal. At one extreme it is possible to find highly detailed exploded-view drawings with every feature, whether the actual subject of the inventive step or not, clearly numbered, and sometimes labelled. At the other end of the scale it is all too easy to find patents which have drawings transferred directly from the back of the proverbial envelope – sketchy, indistinct and inadequately numbered.

In between these extremes are drawings prepared with varying degrees of competence and execution, and in the main they are perfectly suitable for a clear understanding of the text. The variations in quality do affect the way searches are received, for presentation is an important aspect of disclosure, and the ideas most likely to register are the ones which make the fewest demands on the reader's patience. Part of the difference in the quality of presentation is the extent of the back-up facilities available to the applicant. A worker in a large organization can have prepared as many drawings as he feels necessary, with whatever amount of detail he regards as appropriate. The person working for a small organization or on his own has to consider costs much more carefully, and, particularly in the early stages of a project, may elect to try and get by with the minimum amount of graphical detail.

Language, too, varies from the crispness of a closely detailed description complete with a numerical list of parts, to a text full of generalities. A frequently used expression is 'means', as in 'means for fastening' instead of specific terms such as 'screws', 'rivets' or 'bolts'. Such a general approach is understandable, given the inventor's desire to make the patent claims as broad as possible, but the practice does not make for easy reading.

It will be argued that since patents are primarily written to be understood by persons skilled in the art, such a practice presents few real problems. However, given the ever greater degree of specialization among experts, to the point where even in the same broad discipline, co-workers have difficulties understanding each other's terminology, the lack of lucidity can still create very real obstacles to a clear conception of the ideas revealed.

The point is often made that patents are not workshop manuals or instruction leaflets – a fact which is sometimes used to explain the absence of dimensions and other numerical data. Nevertheless, engineers and scientists often cite the absence of such data as one of the reasons why patents have come to be regarded as sources of information which are difficult to use. It is true that references to pressures, temperatures, speeds and tolerances do feature in patents, but not in a consistent and regular fashion.

A further limitation lies in the fact that the store of information represented by patents has been dictated by the purposes for which the patent system was originally conceived, especially the requirement that ideas must be capable of industrial exploitation. Such a requirement generally eliminates topics related to a technology which has an emphasis on theory or speculation. In conventionally published literature, the discussion of theory and practice go hand-in-hand, and ideas can be aired simply to stimulate debate and speculation, and to provoke reaction.

In patents, the rounded view is generally absent – for example, a collection of specifications on valve mechanisms for combustion engines will certainly touch upon basic principles, but the picture which emerges will be one complementary to that appearing in the rest of the literature. Detail after detail will be presented, enabling a composite account to be built up which then has to be assessed against a larger, more balanced body of knowledge and theory. Moreover, many of the ideas disclosed may not be practical for cost reasons, or the absence of suitable materials, or because they are too complex to be reliable. If ideas do possess such negative qualities they will not be exploited commercially and will doubtless soon be forgotten. However, they still form part of the patent literature, and when statements are advanced that a high percentage of information contained in patents is not published in any other form, the reason may be that such information would not stand the scrutiny of a refereed journal, or meet the criteria of a commercially published magazine. The most exposure such ideas can hope for is a paragraph or two in a review article which looks at a whole range of patents relating to a specific technology, and then tries to identify the few that may be of lasting interest.

From the above it will be seen that the picture of a given technology which emerges is uneven, fragmented and greatly in need of careful interpretation and evaluation. Hence the importance of the role of the engineer or information expert specializing in patents. Only by the use of such qualified intermediaries can the full potential of patents as a source of information be fully exploited.

Detailed statistical evidence on the importance of current patents as sources of information in different branches of engineering can be obtained by examining annual figures, such as those published by the European Patent Office, which show numbers of applications arranged by technology units of the International Patent Classification. For 1989, out of a total of 57 765 applications from all countries, the top five technical groups were:

Classes	Applications	Percentage
Instruments I G01-G03	5553	9.61
Electric techniques H01 H02 H05	5207	9.01
Organic chemistry C07 AOI N	4466	7.73
Electronics and communications H03 H04	2981	5.16
Macromolecular compounds C08	2916	5.05
	21122	36.56

Relationship with published literature

The relationship of patents with conventionally published engineering literature crops up in three main ways. Firstly, the inventor, in seeking to sketch the prior art, will use the introductory part of a patent to illustrate earlier developments by citing and quoting from earlier patents and published books, papers and other sources. The amount of detail and the degree of thoroughness will vary a great deal from country to country, with the United States long enjoying a reputation for meticulous and comprehensive recitals.

The objective is to set the scene for the idea disclosed in the specification by explaining how things stood before the inventor made his discovery. The manner in which references are made to earlier publications varies a great deal – some specifications will provide only the briefest of titles, whilst others will quote every detail right down to the ISBN and the publisher's name and address. Such inconsistencies of presentation and style may matter little to the owners and exploiters of a patent, for they are principally concerned with maintaining and enjoying the protection the specification affords, but nevertheless such inconsistencies are yet another reason why patents are seen as less than satisfactory regular sources of technical information.

Standards are available for the correct citation of references to published materials, notably BS 1629:1989,[6] which gives guidance on the form of reference to monographs, serials and contributions, computer software and databases, and indeed patent documents themselves.

Secondly of course, references to the conventional literature occur in official search reports, and again standards of presentation vary. The approaches adopted by different patenting authorities are considered elsewhere in this work (see in particular the comments on the search reports compiled for European and for Patent Cooperation Treaty applications).

So far the relationships between patents and other published documents which have been touched upon may be regarded as internal, in the sense that the references form part of the patent procedure itself. A third relationship exists, in that a few abstracting journals devoted to published engineering sources do make some mention of patents. Of these services, *Chemical Abstracts* is probably the best known for its comprehensive inclusion of patents, and its scope takes in both chemical and chemical engineering specifications from all the major patenting authorities. The quantity of items abstracted in each volume of *Chemical Abstracts* is sufficient to warrant a separate *Patent Index*, a compilation which replaces the *CA Numerical Patent Index* and the *CA Patent Concordance*. The *Patent Index* includes entries for all newly abstracted patent documents on an invention, cross-references to the first abstracted document on an invention when more than one patent document describes that invention, and a listing at the first abstracted document on a particular invention, of all the related patent documents. The primary order of entries is alphabetical by the two-character code for the country of issue, and under each country the patent documents are listed in numerical order.

The treatment accorded to patents by *Chemical Abstracts* is exceptional. *Engineering Index*, for example, makes no reference at all to patents. Similarly the three components of *Science Abstracts*, namely *Physics Abstracts*, *Electrical and Electronic Abstracts*, and *Computer and Control Abstracts*, all covering areas of technology in which inventors are active, do not deal with patents either.

Current-awareness publications devoted exclusively or partially to the reports literature also known as the grey literature,[7] such as *Scientific and Technical Aerospace Reports* (STAR), *Energy Research Abstracts* (ERA) and *Government Reports Announcements and Index* (GRA&I), each carry a fair number of abstracts of patents, albeit without the benefit of drawings or diagrams. In the main, however, entries are confined to abstracts of patent applications and granted patents relating to inventions owned by the United States government.

In addition, the National Technical Information Service (NTIS) issues an annual *Catalog of Government Inventions Available for Licensing*,[8] which covers more than 1000 inventions announced each year, arranged under 43 separate subject headings.

Disclosure systems

A further way of making available details of patentable ideas is through publications known as disclosure journals, the object of which is to make public ideas which are not thought worth the effort of securing patent protection. Such a preemptive approach means that the inventions so revealed can be cited as part of the prior art, and thus cannot be patented by others. Many disclosure journals are published by companies with large research and development facilities, as for example, IBM's *IBM Technical Disclosure Bulletin*, which reveals around 1000 ideas a year through this medium. Other organizations and companies to use the disclosure system include British Rail, Marathon Oil and Xerox.

In addition, it is possible to have a disclosure published for a fee, anonymously, if desired. Two journals providing such a service are *Research Disclosure* and *International Technology Disclosures*, both of which are scanned for the regular inclusion of items in the *World Patents Index*.

Yet another method of revealing details of inventions is embodied in two aspects of practice in the United States which relate to disclosure. Firstly, under its Disclosure Document Program, the US Patent and Trademark Office accepts and preserves, for a 2-year period, papers disclosing an invention pending the filing of a patent application. This disclosure is accepted as evidence of the dates of conception of the invention, but provides no patent protection. The original documents disclosing the idea are kept at the Patent Office for 2 years and then destroyed, unless referred to in a separate letter in a related patent application.

Secondly, the United States Office runs a formal scheme of publishing disclosures, that is, summaries of inventions which act as prior art and therefore prevent anyone else from protecting them. No positive cover results, only the negative advantage of refuge from another's inventiveness. An inventor might publish defensively if he felt that his idea was too small or too similar to another, or if he did not wish to develop it further.

Such revelations are termed Statutory Inventions and at one time were known as Defensives. The documents in question are designated H Specifications and have been appearing since late 1985; by October 1990 the total had reached over 800 disclosures. Names of applicants to whom Statutory Invention Registrations are issued are announced in the *Official Gazette*, as, for example: Conkle, J.P. and Sear, W.J. to United States of America Air Force. Chemical protective balaclava H 823.

References

1   Anthony, L.J. (ed) (1985) *Information sources in engineering*, 2nd edn. London: Butterworths

2   Bain and Co. (1990) *Innovation in Britain today: how major companies can help innovation – and themselves.* London: Bain and Co.
3   The flying sub makes waves in navy circles (1990). *Sunday Correspondent*, 21 October, p. 27
4   Inventor can built space stations made of triangles. (1990) *Daily Telegraph*, 24 September, p. 9 (GB 1512643 filed in 1984)
5   Cold fusion patent claim 'premature' (1990). *Daily Telegraph*, 1 March. See also: Close, F. (1990) *Too hot to handle: the race for cold fusion.* London: W.H. Allen The patent was filed as WO 90/10935
6   British Standards Institution (1989). *Recommendations for references to published materials.* London: BSI (BS 1629:1989)
7   Auger, C.P. (1989) *Information sources in grey literature.* London: Bowker-Saur
8   Center for the Utilization of Federal Technology (1990). *Catalog of government inventions available for licensing.* Springfield, Va: National Technical Information service (PB90-10447CAU). Published annually

CHAPTER ELEVEN

The importance of chemical patents

P.R. STEELE

Introduction

Patents are of great technical and economic importance in the chemical industry generally, and particularly within the pharmaceutical sector. The main reasons for this are the 'copyability' of the products, and the high risk in discovering and developing entities with commercial potential.

For present purposes the term 'chemical patent' is defined with reference to the classification used in the *World Patent Index* (WPI) published by Derwent Publications Ltd. Within WPI, patents are classified as 'chemical', 'mechanical' or 'electrical', with a small number of cases falling into more than one category; the 'chemical' cases constitute a distinct subset of WPI known as the *Chemical Patents Index* (CPI). However, the present definition is even further specialized, comprising only Sections B (pharmaceuticals), C (agrochemicals) and E (general chemicals) of CPI, hence such 'fringe' areas of chemistry as food, textiles, printing and explosives are excluded. The patents making up these three sections of CPI account for only about 11% of all published inventions (see Table 11.1), but deserve this special consideration in view of the specific provisions which have to be made for them, both in legal terms and in terms of the information techniques associated with them.

The chemical industries are involved in the search for new products which will perform some new useful function, or which will perform an existing function more efficiently. Once the utility of a product has been discovered and its safety demonstrated, it becomes a relatively inexpensive task for would-be imitators to copy the product; many useful commercial chemicals could quite literally be produced in realistic quan-

Table 11.1 Chemical patents in World Patents Index in 1990, out of a total of 382383 cases (inventions) in WPI in 1990.

	Total cases in section	Total new compound (NCE) cases	NCE cases as % of section total
Section B (pharmaceutical)	16 858	5780	34%
Section C (agrochemical)	5728	1729	30%
Section E (general chemicals)	24 102	2513	10%
OVERALL:			
Sections BCE (all chemicals - NB overlap)	42 547	8846	21%

tities in a domestic kitchen. Hence in the pharmaceutical industry, for example, the quest is invariably for novel chemical entities or NCEs, which are protectable by means of a so called 'product claim', the strongest type of protection. Other types of claim can sometimes provide comparable protection, as discussed in the section on patent law.

Table 11.1 shows that within the pharmaceutical and agrochemical fields, over 30% of patents are claiming NCEs, whereas in 'general' chemistry (solvents, dyes, intermediates, etc.) this proportion falls to around 10%.

The need for strong patent protection, resulting in an assured monopoly, is compounded in the pharmaceutical industry by the stringent and costly regulatory procedures which necessarily precede the marketing of a new entity, or even a reformulated product. The entire testing and regulatory period is unlikely to be less than 5 years from first synthesis of a potential new drug substance, and can quite commonly be 10 years or more, such is the complexity of the process. Needless to say, the costs incurred are enormous.

A further factor is the high dropout rate in bringing new chemical products to the market. In 1990, for example, it is estimated that 43 NCEs reached the market worldwide as pharmaceutical products[1]. It is more difficult to estimate the number of compounds which had to be synthesized in order to yield these 43 successful entities, but it is certainly of the order of hundreds of thousands, possibly millions, given that a typical pharmaceutical NCE patent (of which there are some 6000 each year) exemplifies several dozen compounds, and that many synthetic programmes fail to yield a patentable (useful) product.

These twin factors, 'copyability' and risk, give rise to an industry which is very vigilant on intellectual property matters. The argument is that without the assurance of a period of competition-free marketing, the massive R&D expenditure simply cannot be justified. Hence the UK pharmaceutical industry, for example, lobbies vigorously through its trade association, the Association of the British Pharmaceutical Industry (ABPI), when changes to patent legislation are under consideration, with a view to maximizing patent protection for the industry's emerging products. Similarly, the Centre for Medicines Research, has as one of its main objectives the study of the erosion of the effective terms pharmaceutical patents, due to so-called 'regulatory delay'. The interplay between industry and government is mentioned later, when various aspects of patent law are considered.

By the same token, individual pharmaceutical companies go to great lengths to obtain patents on their inventions and to enforce those patents. As a result, pharmaceutical patents are more likely than others to become the subject of litigation. In recent years, 'generic' pharmaceutical companies have come to prominence, specializing in the marketing of successful entities in unbranded form as soon as the originator's patents have expired; this aspect, too, has generated considerable litigious activity.

These special features of the pharmaceutical industry play an important part in shaping the relevant patent literature, and must be taken into account when interpreting that literature, as discussed below. Elsewhere in the chemicals sector, for example in the veterinary and agrochemicals industries, some of the same considerations apply, although, arguably, patents are nowhere of more critical importance than in the pharmaceutical industry.

The nature of the pharmaceutical industry

It may be helpful at this stage to summarize the way in which the pharmaceutical industry functions, partly in order to define terminology which will be used later on. The stages through which a typical pharmaceutical product might progress include:

- Identification of biological model of disease
- Chemical synthesis*
- Screening (*in vitro/in vivo*)
- Pharmacology (preclinical)
- Toxicology

- Pharmacokinetic studies (bioavailability)
- Scale-up (pilot plant)[*]
- Formulation[*]
- Clinical trial certificate
- Clinical trials (phases I, II, III, IV)
- Product licence
- Launch
- Post-marketing surveillance
- Licensing
- Relaunch (routes, indications, posology, combinations)[*]
- Parallel importation
- 'Piracy' (infringement)
- Line extensions[*]
- Patent term restoration/marketing exclusivity
- Generic competition[*]

This list, which is not exhaustive, typically encompasses a time scale of 30 years or more, and includes several stages where patents may become of critical importance (indicated by an asterisk). Strictly speaking, it would be more correct to consider here not only patents, but intellectual property generally, of which patents form only a part. A pharmaceutical product may be protectable by a whole range of intellectual property devices, statutory and otherwise, including patents, trademarks, registered designs and copyright; furthermore, pharmaceuticals can sometimes derive protection from other areas of statute law, for example competition law. The wider legal context suggested by these comments should be borne in mind, but detailed discussion in this chapter will be confined to patents.

In other sectors of the chemical industry, many of these same activities will be observed in the typical product lifecycle, but it is in the pharmaceutical industry that patent activity reaches the greatest intensity, due to the stringent safety requirements on the one hand, and the rich rewards for successful products on the other.

Synthesis normally takes place in-house, but sometimes outside specialist laboratories or academic institutions are contracted to produce new compounds, as a way of boosting throughput. As indicated above, tens or hundreds of thousands of compounds may have to be synthesized before a useful product is found, and even a large company may have to wait several years between marketable discoveries. The new compounds are subjected to screening, that is, they are put through tests designed to demonstrate effectiveness or otherwise in a particular disease state. If a new screen is developed, older compounds may be resubmitted. Ideally, patent applications would be filed as the basis for protecting all newly synthesized compounds, but in practice the patent agent, in consultation with research scientists, seeks protection only for those which show some promise in early screens. Any delay in filing the initial patent application could result in loss of novelty, due to a publication. However, the subsequent, more detailed pharmacology, toxicology and pharmacokinetic studies may demonstrate that some, or even all, of the new compounds in an initial patent application are in fact useless for one reason or another. Thus, when the time comes a year later to 'complete' the patent application (add claims and file abroad, as explained elsewhere), many cases may simply be dropped; practice varies from company to company, but observation suggests that a typical UK-based multinational completes only about 10% of its original filings. This patent application claiming an NCE is known colloquially as the 'product case'.

Two general comments as to the nature of this initial pharmaceutical patenting activity may now be appropriate. First, almost all worthwhile patenting of pharmaceutical NCEs originates from multinationals, and their patenting is itself international; all inventions perceived to show commercial potential will be filed in 20 or so major markets (Europe, Japan, USA), whilst cases of exceptional promise might cover 30 or 40 or even more territories worldwide. Secondly, the world pharmaceuticals market is surprisingly fragmented (and therefore competitive) compared with other industries, such that the very biggest companies struggle to achieve even 3% of total sales; historically, through the 1970s and 1980s, European-based companies (especially those in the UK) have consistently discovered (and patented) more significant new products than would be predicted from their size or market share.

As development of a new product begins to get under way there is likely to be a succession of process and formulation patents from the originator, as bulk material is required for more extensive testing, first possibly in animals (preclinical), but then in clinical trials. The point about this second wave of patent activity is that the product case itself, filed with almost indecent haste within a few weeks of synthesis, may not have addressed the practical problems of producing useful quantities of the compound by safe and efficient means, or of formulating it into tablets, for example, which have an acceptable shelf life. The specification of the product case will include *a* workable synthetic process and will suggest *a* formulation suitable for administration (these are basic patentability requirements), but these early laboratory methods will almost certainly turn out to be unsuitable for operation on a commercial scale, where tonne quantities (hopefully!) and robust dosage forms will be required.

Patent activity may then subside for a year or two while trial data are produced and analyzed and international registration dossiers are prepared with a view to satisfying the regulatory authorities as to the safety and efficacy of the intended new product. In the UK the end product of this activity, if successful, is a product licence (on no account to be confused with a patent licence) and the process is overseen by the Medicines Commission and the Committee on Safety of Medicines (CSM). In the USA it is the Food and Drug Administration (FDA) which has the equivalent responsibility to grant IND (investigational new drug) status, leading through to an NDA (new drug application); there is also an Abbreviated NDA (ANDA), but this should not be confused with a CANDA (computer-assisted NDA) – merely a symptom of the huge quantities of paper which this regulatory activity can produce! It is not the intention here to go deeply into regulatory procedures or jargon, but a basic familiarity with these concepts is becoming necessary as a result of the growing interdependence between patent life and the dates of regulatory approval and marketing.

The launch date of a pharmaceutical product, is typically 8–12 years after first synthesis, but variations well outside this range are not unusual; it would be difficult to bring a product to market in much less than 5 years, but at the other end of the scale a product could conceivably be launched even after expiry of the product patent, perhaps due to the patentee's lack of diligence, or more likely as a result of technical or commercial problems.

What follows next, commercially and in patent terms, is highly unpredictable. Assuming that the product survives its first year or two (some quickly flop and subside into oblivion!) there are opportunities for licensing, relaunching, parallel importation, infringement and line extension, for example. There are numerous situations which may arise which have patent and associated litigation implications.

Licensing was traditionally resorted to by the smaller pharmaceutical companies, when they recognized their inability fully to exploit one of their patented inventions, either because of a territorial marketing weakness or because of insufficient experience in a particular therapeutic area. Recently, however, licensing, cross-licensing, joint ventures, co-marketing and even co-promotion (same brand name, same market) have become the order of the day, and such activities involve the very biggest companies in pairings which a few years ago would have suggested only arch-rivalry. This is simply evidence of an intensely competitive specialized market, with no dominant companies. Almost always these arrangements will involve patent licences, although it is relatively unusual for the details (or even the existence) of these to become public knowledge.

If the product is a so-called 'blockbuster', within a year or so of launch it will attract the attention of other companies who wish to capitalize on its success. This they attempt to do by applying for patents relating to aspects of the successful product – at a time when the originator of the product is probably concentrating on marketing rather than innovation. These third parties, which often include small companies, may be claiming new uses for the product, new processes, new formulations, a mixture with their existing product, and so on. They cannot of course exploit their inventions immediately, and so at first their motivation for patenting may seem puzzling. One possibility is that they are simply lining up a protected product for the day when the originator's product case finally expires, but more likely they are hoping for a cross-licence arrangement, whereby the originator receives rights to the new development and grants the innovator rights to the original entity. Whatever the underlying motivation, this outburst of 'me-too' patenting by third parties during the years following launch is a characteristic of the patent profile for many of the top-selling pharmaceuticals from the past two decades.

The originator may at some stage decide to revitalize the product, possibly by claiming new indications, by reducing the dosage frequency or by improving the mode of administration or compliance, and of course patenting will result. This 'line extension' is most likely to happen during the last few years of the product patent life. The originator recognizes that shortly it will be possible for any competent company to launch a product based on the original, as disclosed in the product case, and so resolves to update (and patent) the product. On product patent expiry the imitator can get approval relatively easily to sell what is, effectively, a copy of the original, taking advantage of abbreviated regulatory procedures. However, he cannot get access to the updated formulation, or for that matter to the originator's trade name – hence these companies generally sell under the approved or generic name of the active chemical entity. Some multinationals, recognizing the potentially dramatic drop in revenue which can result from patent expiry on a 'blockbuster', now have their own generics division or subsidiary, to ensure that they keep as much as possible of their lucrative market following expiry.

Patented products can also be subject to parallel importation, and again, the temptation is considerable for smaller companies, not necessarily even pharmaceutical companies, where big products are involved. The onus is generally on the patent owner to detect and prove infringement, and clearly there is very little point in having the patent property in the first place unless there is a commitment and capability to do this. Tracking down an infringer often involves inquiries which lead back to non-developed markets where patent laws are weak or unenforceable, but from where material is being moved into markets where enforcement becomes both possible and desirable. Parallel importation is more difficult to tackle on the basis of patent rights alone, since free trade legislation often dominates, but copyright in packs and package inserts has sometimes provided protection.

Patent laws – special provisions for chemicals and pharmaceuticals

Having charted the progress of a drug from synthesis to patent expiry and noted significant patent events, it may now be appropriate to look in more detail at some of the special provisions which exist:

Types of claim

Almost 200 territories have patent laws, but there is considerable variety in the provisions they make for pharmaceuticals. There are also various regional groupings and conventions, tending further to complicate the picture; of greatest significance are the Paris Convention, the Patent Co-operation Treaty (PCT) and the European Patent Convention (EPC), but even within these groupings there is a lack of uniformity.

Furthermore, the position is far from static, with changes occurring in the overall picture several times each year; hence textbooks are not a great deal of use in this area. Hans Scheer Verlag produce a frequently updated wallchart summarizing the main types of protection in 56 major countries, and a diskette spreadsheet version now also exists for use on PCs. However, looseleaf publications give the most detailed accounts, and Baxter[2] suggests that there is a tendency for the laws of industrial countries to move towards giving more protection to pharmaceuticals, whereas in developing countries the reverse is generally true. The same source adds a caveat to the effect that when it comes to deciding exactly what is or is not patentable in a particular country, practice may vary from examiner to examiner.

Baxter looks on a country-by-country basis at the possibilities for obtaining the following six types of claims:

- Processes for making chemical compounds
- Chemical compounds which are pharmaceuticals
- Non-pharmaceuticals (i.e. intermediates or other utilities)
- Pharmaceutical compositions
- Methods of making pharmaceutical compositions
- Methods for therapeutically treating humans with pharmaceuticals

In a separate tabulation the related questions of patentability of biological processes and the resulting products are dealt with.

The USA, for example, permits claims to all eight of the categories mentioned above. The UK however traditionally does not allow claims to methods of treating humans, or to the product of a biological process, unless that process involves a microorganism which has been deposited in an official collection. Within the EPC, neither Spain nor Greece at present allows claims to pharmaceutical products *per se*, and hence there would normally be a separate set of process-only claims for these territories at the end of a European patent application.

At the other end of the spectrum, countries such as Bolivia, Czechoslovakia and India recognize only two or three of the types of claim which interest the pharmaceutical industry.

Two oddities of emerging technology may perhaps be of interest here. First, within the rapidly evolving biotechnology field, there is the question of whether new, genetically engineered life forms are patentable; recently granted cases such as US 4736866 (the 'Harvard mouse' patent) suggest that they are indeed patentable[3]. Secondly, as a consequence of the Washington Research Foundation's US 4966911[4], it seems now to be possible to claim a pharmacophore, that is a molecule defined not in terms of its atoms and bonds but in terms of binding groups and their spatial relationships, determining their ability to block or activate a biological receptor.

Filing lists

From the above, it will be clear that in some less developed countries a pharmaceutical company will find it difficult or impossible to obtain worthwhile patent protection for its products. Furthermore, there is the problem that, however strong the patentee's claims may be, there may not be in existence a competent legal system through which to enforce those claims. Companies therefore decide the number of countries where protection will be sought (the so-called filing list), in terms of their perception of the importance of the invention. Secondary sources of patents information such as WPI or INPADOC include lists of equivalent patents (families), and the implicit information content of these lists should not be overlooked.

Filing list decisions may also to some extent be shaped by local market characteristics. A treatment for frostbite is unlikely to achieve huge sales in the tropics, for example, any more than leishmaniasis cures will be In demand in temperate regions. Less predictably, racial groupings exhibit predilections for particular routes of drug administration; the French are known to favour the use of suppositories, whereas the Japanese seem to like the idea of percutaneous administration, employing impregnated patches and plasters.

Compulsory licences

The UK Patents Act 1977 Section 1(3)(a) defines as unpatentable anything which might .... encourage offensive, immoral or antisocial
behaviour. Conversely, there seems always to have been a feeling that
anything which is particularly good for society, such as a therapeutic or
nutritious product, should be protectable, but must not be the subject of
an unreasonable monopoly; the Parker Committee in 1916, for example,
stated that 'Food, drugs and medicinal and chemical preparations are all
of such extreme value to the public that no obstructive patent ought to be
allowed'[5]. One result of this is that the laws of many countries contain
special provisions for the compulsory licensing of pharmaceuticals.

Voluntary licensing is common in the pharmaceutical industry, for the
types of reason alluded to above; the licensee pays an agreed royalty in
return for specified rights in stated territories. Information on such licences often does not appear on the public record, but the UK Patents Act
1949 Section 41 gave the Comptroller of the Patent Office power to grant
a licence to interested persons for 'a substance capable of being used as
food or medicine .... on such terms as he thinks fit ....' This is the compulsory licence provision; no doubt to the relief of the pharmaceutical
industry, very little use was made of Section 41, and there is no equivalent provision explicitly for drugs in the 1977 Act. However, in former
Commonwealth territories whose patent laws are based upon earlier British laws, such as Canada and New Zealand, such compulsory licence
provisions still remain. In Canada in particular, considerable advantage
has been taken of their Section 41 by indigenous chemical companies,
and over 1000 such licences in respect of major products have now been
imposed upon multinationals on this basis.

In the Netherlands, Section 34 contains a rather different compulsory
licence (strictly cross-licence) provision, whereby the owner of a process
patent, for example, can demand from the product patent owner the rights
needed to enable him to exercise his (process) invention. Similar provisions exist in Scandinavia.

Licences of Right

A related UK concept is the Licences of Right endorsement. This too has
taken on a special significance for pharmaceutical patents in recent years,
but should not be confused with the compulsory licence provisions
referred to above.

Originally, the principal use of the Licences of Right endorsement
(UK Patents Act 1949, Section 35) was to allow the owner to make a patent freely available for licensing at an agreed royalty rate. A patent
voluntarily endorsed in this way became subject to payment of renewal
fees at only half the normal rate, and so in practice this device, which is

reversible retrospectively, was often used to keep an unused patent in force more cheaply, rather than allowing it to lapse irrevocably.

However, with the Patents Act 1977 the term Licences of Right assumed a new significance in that all 'new existing' patents, as defined in Schedule 1 of that Act, were so endorsed during the last 4 years of their term. In effect, this meant that any patent with a UK filing date from June 1967 to May 1978 inclusive had its term extended automatically from 16 to 20 years, but was subject to 'involuntary' Licences of Right endorsement during that 4-year extension.

This provision applies to all new existing patents, regardless of subject matter, but has been particularly contentious with respect to pharmaceutical patents. A successful drug product will have been on the market typically for only 6 – 8 years when it reaches its 'original' 16-year expiry point, and because of its high sales will be very attractive to potential generic competitors. (The same would not be true of many other industries, for example electronics, where the dynamics of product development are different, since commercial interest in the product will be negligible by the time expiry occurs).

Many smaller chemical companies were therefore keen to take advantage of the Licences of Right provided by this 1977 Act transitional arrangement, since they could thereby gain access to valuable generic pharmaceutical markets 4 years earlier than would otherwise be possible. Details of these licences do not necessarily become public, but there is provision in Section 46(3) of the Act for the Comptroller of the Patent Office to intervene if the parties cannot agree the terms of a licence, and these interventions are reported in the *Official Journal (Patents)*. Status Information in INPADOC suggests that up to the beginning of 1991 some 121 Section 46(3) proceedings had been notified, and no less than 87 of these relate to pharmaceutical patents, a clear indication of the importance of this provision for the industry. In several instances, the dispute over licence terms was not satisfactorily settled by the Comptroller, and cases then came before the High Court, Court of Appeal and House of Lords. Apart from setting the royalty rate and mechanism, these cases were concerned also with supply routes, in particular the licensee's freedom to import raw material rather than buy supplies from the licensor. One of the key cases related to salbutamol, the asthma drug sold by Glaxo as Ventolin[6].

That arrangement should have run for 11 years, from June 1987 (the true expiry date of the earliest 'new existing' patent) until the first of the 1977 Act expiries, in June 1998. In fact the pharmaceutical industry lobbied vigorously, and effectively put an end to pharmaceutical Licences of Right in January 1990. From that date, under the terms of the Copyright, Designs and Patents Act 1988 (Section 293) a declaration may be filed stating that a licence is *not* available as of right for an excepted use. Such declarations are valid for patents relating to medicinal products, within the meaning of the Medicines Act 1968. However, of 769 cases subjected to declarations filed on this basis up to early 1991, only about 85% are clearly pharmaceutical; the remainder are mainly agrochemical, there being a similar excepted use provision for such products, though with a rather later implementation date.

The licences of right saga will not finally be resolved until the new law expiries begin in 1998; other European countries entering the EPC system in 1978 adopted their own transitional arrangements, but nowhere has there been the uncertainty and litigation which the UK 1977 Act generated.

Extensions

For any patent there will be a 'normal' expiry date, which may be calculated from the date of grant, or more usually, the date of application. A patent can cease to exist (lapse) earlier than this if renewal fees are not paid, but under certain conditions it is also possible in certain countries for the term to be extended. Traditionally, pharmaceutical companies were often able to take advantage of Section 23 of the UK Patent Act 1949, which provided for extensions of 5 (exceptionally 10) years if the patentee could prove 'inadequate remuneration', that is insufficient time on the market to generate profits which would repay development costs; product patents for compounds such as clindamycin, diclofenac, prazosin and tamoxifen were extended in this way. Similar extension provisions still exist in former Commonwealth territories such as South Africa, New Zealand and Australia, but the UK Patents Act 1977 has no such provision. Instead, we are seeing the emergence of extension or 'restoration' provisions more specifically tailored to the pharmaceutical industry, in the sense that they attempt to quantify the regulatory delay to which individual products are subject.

Patent term restoration (PTR)

PTR is closely related to the subjects of patent expiry and generic competition. The pharmaceutical industry has long argued that if the marketing of a product is delayed by the requirement for rigorous testing, then that in itself should not penalize the originator – he should in fact have his patent term topped up (restored) to take into account the regulatory delay incurred. The first country to act on this was the USA, when, in 1984, the so-called Waxman–Hatch legislation came into effect. Like the patent system itself, Waxman–Hatch has the nature of a bargain, in that through the ANDA provision the generic companies receive assistance in obtaining approval on patent-expired products, but the originator can first claim a patent extension of up to 5 years to compensate for regulatory delay. In fact, the calculation follows a particulary tricky algorithm which distinguishes between the testing and regulatory phases (the so-called $\frac{1}{2}$A+B factor) and requires that the applicant has displayed 'due diligence' in progressing the product towards approval. Details of the FDA's calculations on these applications appear in the Federal Register, and the DHHS's *Approved Drug Products* contains an annual listing of expiry dates, with cumulative monthly updates, A final twist is that marketing exclusivity, which limits third parties' access to the ANDA route, can on occasions effectively extend the originator's monopoly beyond expiry of the patent.

PTR measures have also been introduced in Japan and France, and a similar supplementary protection certificate (SPC) is under active consideration in Europe at the time of writing. In the first 3 years' operation of the Japanese provisions (January 1988 – December 1990), the Japanese Pharmaceutical Manufacturers' Association[7] reports that 42 pharmaceutical products received patent term extensions; these averaged just under 7 years, giving an average patent-protected market life of almost 11 years for each product.

The French provisions are less significant, since presumably they will become subordinate to any EEC provision which may emerge from the current SPC debate. European pharmaceutical trade associations and individual companies have been vigorously lobbying with a view to obtaining 16 years' protected marketing for their products, whereas the Commission itself and some national governments have been arguing for lower figures, making comparisons with other markets, including Japan and the USA. Moreover, the European proposal, as it stands, would result in the grant of a supplementary protection certificate rather than a patent extension as such. It remains to be seen exactly what will emerge, but PTR now clearly represents a significant asset for the pharmaceutical industry, and there has been talk of extending the principle into other sectors such as agrochemicals.

It will be clear from the foregoing discussion that patent expiry is the focus of a great deal of interest in the pharmaceutical industry, and that PTR provisions are actively evolving worldwide. It is difficult to do justice to this aspect of the subject in a short space, but a more detailed account has recently appeared[8].

Information needs

The innovatory cycle of the pharmaceutical industry has been described, and some of the consequent special provisions in patent legislation have been considered. Within these contexts, the requirements of the pharmaceutical industry for patents information can now be surveyed, again taking particular note of some special provisions which have been made. Jackson[9] offers an excellent classification of the types of patents searching needed by a pharmaceutical company, distinguishing patent purposes from non-patent (or purely information) requirements.

Searches carried out for patent purposes

Novelty/patentability

Searches are carried out before filing a patent application in order to determine whether the supposed invention is, in fact, novel. A prior relevant publication could destroy novelty by disclosing the essence of the invention, either specifically or generically; the applicant needs to be aware of such publications when deciding exactly how broadly to claim a monopoly. 'Publication' in this context means not only patent specifications, but also journals and less formal sources such as conference papers, newspapers and broadcasts. However, for chemical companies it is disclosures in patent specifications which create the most serious problems, as will be explained.

Validity

Searching may need to be carried out to determine the likely validity of a third party patent, for example if that patent appears to present an obstacle, or if it is under consideration for licensing in. In those countries where careful substantive examination occurs, the examiner is in effect giving his view on validity in deciding the scope of the claims which can be granted. Some countries provide for opposition at the time of grant, but pharmaceutical companies seem to make little use of this, preferring to form an independent view of validity. From the searcher's viewpoint, the validity search is in effect a novelty search relating to a past date – 'Was this invention patentable at the time of filing?'.

Infringement

Any new or reformulated product which is to be marketed could infringe the patent property of a third party, and should therefore be the subject of an infringement or 'clearance' search. Unlike the two previous criteria, this searching is confined to patents, and needs to cover only those cases which are in force in the territories where commercial activity is to be undertaken. An important point to restate here, is that even the possession of a valid in-force patent protecting an invention does not guarantee that the invention is non-infringing – a third party could well have an earlier case with a valid broader claim reading on to the invention.

In practice, the searcher may find that all three types of patent search require the use of the same search techniques and sources, even though assessment of the retrieved patents will need to be matched to the purpose of the search. In any case, one type of search may imply or lead to another. A novelty search may imply an infringement search ('Can we patent this compound, and if so would we be free to sell it?'); an infringement search may lead to a validity search ('This patent seems to prevent us from exploiting our invention, but is it valid?').

PROBLEMS AND SOLUTIONS

Away from the organic chemistry area, the patent information requirements of the chemical industry are largely met by storage and retrieval based on the classification and natural language techniques used in other sectors, and Indeed in literature searching generally. Thus if a chemical manufacturer invents a reaction vessel, or if a drug company wishes to sell a redesigned pack, searching based on the IPC (International Patent Classification) and the text of WPI abstracts may well suffice; the full text of specifications in searchable form is now beginning to be made available through the medium of CD-ROM, and this will make such 'general' searching even more reliable.

However, it is organic chemistry which causes the greatest retrieval problems. Organic molecules vary greatly in structure, and conventional classification schemes are often too coarse to allow the necessary detail to be recorded, even when used in conjunction with indexing schedules; a relatively small optional variation in a molecule could cause it to appear in a completely different place in a hierarchical classification such as the IPC.

When drafting chemical specifications, patent agents now routinely make use of the generalized representation of a molecule which has become known as the 'Markush structure', after Eugene Markush who in 1924 was named as inventor on a generalized dyestuff process patent, US 1506316. (in fact Markush was *not* the originator of generic chemical structures in patents – he simply avoided the use of the word 'or' by introducing the phrase ' ...selected from the group consisting of .... and .... and...'). These Markush structures consist of atoms or groups which are subject to variation, and hence need further definition, typically (but not necessarily) associated with a fixed or essential 'core' to the molecule. The Markush structure in a pharmaceutical or agrochemical new compound case will quite commonly encompass hundreds of thousands of specific entities, sometimes literally an infinite number.

Numerous authors have described the information storage and retrieval problems associated with this so-called 'Markush problem', none more eloquently than Goehring and Sibley,[10] who focus on a particular impossibly broad PCT case, WO 87/04321.

Traditionally, the information scientist requiring information from chemical patents has been heavily dependent on two main secondary sources, *Chemical Abstracts* and WPI. Lynch[11], however, goes on to list over a dozen other contributions to the subject of generic structure handling, several of which have never developed into working retrieval systems.

The *Chemical Abstracts* standard approach has always been based on indexing of specific 'real' compounds reported in the published literature, that is principally those for which physical data are quoted as hard evidence of synthesis; retrieval of these specific compounds is achieved through the use of systematic nomenclature, complemented more recently by a registry system which results in connection-table representations of molecules, these being substructure-searchable via CAS-Online. The specific compound approach is appropriate for working chemists, who normally need practical details of the synthesis and use of compounds. Patent agents, by contrast, need access to *all* compounds falling within broad disclosures or generic claims, since even hypothetical references may have a bearing on the questions of novelty, validity and infringement discussed earlier. *Chemical Abstracts* have therefore devised MARPAT, a system capable of storing the Markush structural information from patents, and for searching it with specific or generic enquiries. The thinking behind MARPAT was outlined by Fisanick[12], who is the inventor named on a subsequent patent[13]. The searchable file begins in 1988, and it is still too early for comprehensive retrieval tests to have been published; however, indications are that reasonably precise retrieval is achievable without substantial loss of recall.

Recognizing the need for Markush structure storage and retrieval, Derwent Publications in 1963 began a service for pharmaceutical companies called FARMDOC, a development of an earlier fine chemicals patents abstracting service. FARMDOC employed a chemical fragment code based on the 80-column x 12-row IBM punched card, which could be passed through an electromechanical card sorter. In concept, the FARMDOC code resembled one developed specifically for steroid patents by the US Patent & Trademark Office in the 1950s, and indeed that code was adapted by Derwent to form a special code within FARMDOC. Coding of all chemical patents in this way began in 1970, when the CPI service was introduced.

The FARMDOC fragment code is empirical (rather than analytical), being based on about 800 ring systems and substituent groups which were commonly found in the types of molecule being patented in the early 1960s. There were catchall 'other' codes for rarer fragments, but certain types of molecule which came to prominence later (prostaglandins, macrolides, polypeptides) were not easy to deal with meaningfully. A Ring Index Number system (developed from the original ACS 'Patterson' system) was added in 1974, and a major revision in 1981 made generic grouping of codes possible, as well as some additional coding for positions of substitution and so on. The success of Derwent's chemical codes has been due to the fact that they reflect the language used in patent specifications, having roughly the same level of specificity. The total recall which lawyers require is, in theory, achievable, but the precision of these fragment code searches is often depressingly low. The searcher may have to scan through the abstracts of 1000 or more 'hits' in order to locate a dozen or so truly relevant answers – the rejects may well have the required fragments present, but either with incorrect connectivity, or in mutually exclusive sets of alternatives. Paradoxically, it was the introduction of online searching of CPI in about 1975 which made this low precision less tolerable; punched cards included a printed Markush structure with definitions, and could very quickly be rejected if they were clearly 'false drops', but the online files had abstracts consisting only of text. Derwent invested heavily in the development of a true Markush storage and retrieval system for CPI, finally launching their Markush DARC (MDARC) file in 1987. Like MARPAT, however, MDARC is still too young to have undergone exhaustive evaluation, as is a related product from the French Patent Office, MPHARM.

It will now be clear that the 'Markush problem' lies at the centre of patents information requirements for the chemical industry. Not only are many chemical patent applications drafted generically, but many enquiries, certainly in the important area of novelty searching, are also expressed in broad generic terms. Imprecise terminology such as 'optionally substituted', 'heterocyclic' and 'pharmaceutically acceptable group' frequently occur in specifications and enquiries alike. Total recall is an absolute requirement on many occasions, preferably with precision approaching 100%. It seems unlikely that either *Chemical Abstracts* or Derwent have yet arrived at the perfect solution to the problem. Furthermore, the problem itself may now need redefining, if patenting of pharmacophores[4] becomes commonplace.

Searches carried out for non-patent purposes

Quite separately from their legal significance, chemical patent specifications constitute a systematic body of scientific and technical literature referring to everything happening in the industry which might have commercial potential. Most patent applications are now published routinely 18 months after first application, and much of the information which they contain will never be published elsewhere. In general, chemical patents can be of value both for the scientific information which they contain, and for the commercial intelligence which, with appropriate analysis, they may yield.

SCIENTIFIC INFORMATION

A patent specification is essentially a working document. The underlying principle, after all, is that inventors should be able to build on the inventions of those already in the field. The applicant must disclose the best method known to him of carrying out the invention; he must demonstrate that it works (not necessarily explaining *why* it works), giving sufficient practical detail to enable the 'person skilled in the art' to reproduce the invention. If such detail is lacking, the patents may be judged invalid on the grounds of 'insufficiency'. Thus a pharmaceutical specification, for example, will normally give methods for synthesizing compounds (with spectral data, melting points and, occasionally, research code numbers), biological test methods and possibly explicit data (activity and toxicity) for the lead compounds, routes of administration and examples of formulations.

Patent references are in fact often retrieved alongside journal references when a search for scientific information is conducted in a 'composite' database, that is one containing both types of primary literature. Patents feature in *Chemical Abstracts*, as discussed above, but also for example in BIOSIS, *Biotechnology Abstracts* and the Chemical Reactions Documentation Service (*Journal of Synthetic Methods*). These specialist secondary services offer the scientist good retrieval facilities by abstracting and indexing patents, with emphasis on those scientific details relevant to the specialism.

Because research in some areas is highly competitive, the need exists to bring certain key patent applications quickly to the attention of research scientists; early awareness of a highly relevant third party publication could prompt a constructive change of direction in a research project, and possibly save days or weeks of wasted synthetic work. In recognition of this need, Current Patents Ltd began producing therapeutic *Fast-Alert* bulletins in 1989, alerting scientists to new specifications from key countries within a week or so of publication; this contrasts with a delay of 3 months to a year or longer incurred by Derwent and *Chemical Abstracts* as they perform their more detailed abstracting and indexing operations, primarily for 'archival' purposes. *Fast-Alert* shows only a specific structure (a preferred one) for each patent, but is now available in diskette form for substructure searching using ChemBase software. An alerting service, *Patent Reviews*, is now available from Derwent too.

COMMERCIAL INTELLIGENCE

Virtually everything which a company patents has commercial potential – that is the motivation for seeking a monopoly. The pharmaceutical industry is highly competitive, and a great deal of effort goes into watching and analyzing competitors' patents in the hope of gaining early warning of forthcoming developments. Promising compounds from these patents might be seen as competition or as licensing prospects, but in either case they cannot be ignored. Specialist secondary sources attempt to cover pharmaceutical patents from this point of view, for example the Pharma-Projects service from PJB and the *Drug Data Report* (DDR) from Prous. PharmaProjects lists products known to be in development, quoting a relevant patent number if this is known, and substructure searching is available in PharmaStructures using Psidom or ChemBase software. DDR approaches from the opposite direction, as it were, in that recent patents are analyzed with a view to identifying the most promising compounds, and again a substructure file exists (ChemBase/MACCS).

At the other end of the drug development cycle, a great deal of significance is attached to patent expiry, and several sources exist giving an indication of the patent status of marketed products. Again, the implications of this patent information cannot be ignored, since the commercial balance (prices, market shares) of an entire therapeutic area can be disrupted when an important entity 'goes off patent' and cheaper generic competition arrives on the scene. A company can gain strategic advantage by anticipating such a change, if not by actually participating in the generic market. Early patents, including the product patent, will not refer to a product by its approved name, but secondary sources such as the *Merck Index* offer a degree of assistance by correlating name with patent number for many products. In practice, a straightforward listing of patent expiry dates against drug names may not be possible, or even sensible. In their Imsworld online file Patents International, IMS offer a carefully checked international expiry date listing, with caveats wherever necessary on possible extensions of term, important formulation cases, and so on; the same file is available via orbit as Drug Patents International. Paltnoi Associates offer a similar service, *European Drug Patent Status Review*, with data for 900 products and accompanying status information.

Summary

Patents have been shown to be particularly important in the chemical industry. This importance derives from the nature of the products, and from their characteristic discovery, development and marketing cycles. Patent laws often make special provision for chemicals, especially pharmaceuticals. Chemical patent specifications, because of their generic nature, create difficult or even insoluble information problems when it comes to their storage and retrieval. The publishing industry is responding by creating more sophisticated and specialized products. The picture is far from settled: in legal terms the next 5 years will see a significant extension of the provisions for patent term restoration, whilst in information retrieval terms attention will continue to focus on the Markush problem.

References

1   Davis, J. (1990) '43 NCE introductions in 1990' *Scrip*, Review Issue, December, 20–21
2   Baxter: *World patent law and practice*. Release 60 (11/88) App. 2–1
3   Leder, P. and Stewart, T.A. (1988) *Transgenic non-human animals*. US Patent 4736866 (priority 22.1.84)
4   Clark, J.I., Far, A.G. and Smith, S.A. (Washington Research Foundation) (1990) *Immunoregulatory agents*. US Patent 4966911 (priority 20.11.84)
5   *Proposed amendments to the Patents and Designs Act 1907* (The 'Parker Report') 1916
6   Allen and Hanburys Ltd's (salbutamol) patent (1987) *Reports ... of patent cases* RPC 327.
7   Products which gained patent extension in Japan. *Scrip*, no 1604-5 April 3-5, 1991.
8   Redwood, H. (1990) *Pharmaceutical patent term restoration for the 1990s*. Suffolk: Oldwicks Press
9   Jackson, S.E. (1984) Experiences of a patents searcher. In: *Computer handling of generic chemical structures*, ed. by J.M. Barnard. Proceedings, CSA Conference, Sheffield, 26–29 March 1984. Aldershot: Gower, pp. 30–37
10   Goehring, K.E.H. and Sibley, J.F. (1989) 'A giant step for mankind?' *World Patent Information*, **11**, 5–10
11   Lynch, M.F. (1984) *Introduction*. In: Barnard, J.M. op. cit.[9] pp. 1–10
12   Fisanick, W. (1984) *Requirements for a system for storage and search of Markush structures*. In: Barnard, J.M. *op. cit*[9]. 106-129.
13   Fisanick, W. (1987) *Storage and retrieval of generic chemical structure representations*. US Patent 4642762 (priority 25.5.84)

Editor's note: The broader aspects of the pharmaceutical industry's information activities are covered in: Pickering, W.R. (ed) (1990) *Information sources in pharmaceuticals*. London: Bowker-Saur

CHAPTER TWELVE

Patenting in the life sciences

N.J. Byrne

Life is a complex matter. Where, and indeed how, life began, and what we understand by life, are deeply philosophical, not to say highly controversial, issues that have been debated vigorously for centuries. A new dimension to the debate about life and its meaning has come in the wake of advances in the biological sciences during the past 20 years. These advances enable scientists to create, and recreate, life-forms not previously known to humanity, such as the goat–sheep chimera (or 'geep'), the featherless chicken, and the 'ice-minus' bacterium. But this newly developed ability has fostered a volatile opposition to 'those who would play God'; an opposition that regards the availability of patents for new life creating processes and for living things 'engineered' using the techniques of the new biology, as encouraging activities that, in the end, could be fatal for life. The various nightmare scenarios envisaged by opponents of 'patents on life', and the ethics surrounding this, can be left aside for others to question.

The task in this chapter is less ambitious. It is to examine some of the unique administrative issues posed for the patent system by the complexities of animate inventions, and in particular, to discuss the legal requirement for a 'reproducible' description, a precondition for the grant of a patent. For the inventor of an inanimate artefact or a manufacturing process that uses 'dead' materials, this requirement ordinarily presents no real difficulty. The construction of a particular mousetrap can be described easily in words, aided perhaps by a drawing. However, words alone may be incapable of describing how to 'make' or 'reproduce' a particular mouse.

The problem with plants

The extreme difficulty, if not sheer impossibility, of giving a reproducible (or enabling) description for a new plant was recognized in the 1920s in the USA, and has been widely discussed since then.[1] In earlier years, the difficulty went unrecognized, or at least it seems not to have excited any great concern in the literature of patent law, when patents were granted for microbiological inventions. Louis Pasteur was granted a United States patent (US 141 072) in 1873 for a yeast, free from organic germs of disease, used in beer fermentation. Other patents were issued in the USA in the late 1800s on bacterial and viral vaccines.

Earlier still, though outside the USA, in 1833 Pope Gregory decreed that the breeder or finder of a new plant was entitled to exclusive rights in respect of the plant within the precincts of Saint Peter's Patrimony. No doubt the 1833 decree had some implicit, if not an express, requirement for a practical means of identifying the new plant, so that the breeder or finder could claim what the decree entitled him to. The decree may have required the breeder to maintain a reference sample of what he claimed as his new plant.

A description of a plant, an animal or a microorganism may allow a skilled biologist or taxonomist to identify the organism. However, the modern patent system sets a far more exacting standard for patent applicants. A patent specification must describe the invention in terms complete enough to enable a person skilled in the particular art to reproduce the claimed invention. In the context of plant breeding, the requirement for an reproducible description was recognized as practically impossible, if not altogether wholly inappropriate, by the US Plant Patent Act 1930.[2] It remains an impossible criterion to meet because, if another plant breeder were to repeat the well known steps in conventional plant breeding – hybridization between compatible parents followed by selection from a highly variable population – it is not probable, indeed it may be highly improbable, that he or she would arrive at the same result again; and an inappropriate condition because, when a new plant has been bred, seldom will another plant breeder want to breed that plant. It has been estimated, for example, that if two plants that differ in only 21 gene pairs are crossed and a selection is made from the resulting progeny, the probability of repeating the selection is 2 in 4 399 046 511 104. But who can deny that within the next decade or two, advances in the biological sciences may allow the plant breeder or the animal breeder to give a reproducible description as easily as the industrial chemist.

The deposit solution for microorganisms

The difficulties inherent in the legal requirement for a reproducible description led the US Act of 1930 to relax this requirement for new plants, by permitting the description to be in accordance with traditional botanical descriptions. To date, some 6000 US patents have been issued under the 1930 Act. These are relatively short documents. A plant patent specification identifies (by means of a botanical description and a coloured drawing) the variety protected by the patent. It is not, in the way that an industrial patent specification purports to be, a teaching document addressed to persons skilled in the art.

Inventors in the field of microbiology, when they began patenting microbiological processes, presented patent offices throughout the industrial world with a problem similar to that set by the plant breeder. A strain of microorganism might have been isolated from a soil sample or a dung heap, purified in the laboratory, and then used for the production of a valuable antibiotic. But it might avail a skilled person nothing if, in an effort to reproduce the same microorganism, he or she followed the procedures detailed in a patent specification. The inventor may have had a 'lucky dip', and the odds against repeating this might be astronomical[3]. For this reason, in the late 1940s the US Patent Office began to insist, as a condition for the granting of a patent where the invention depended on the use of a microorganism *not already available to the public*, that the applicant deposited a sample of the organism in a reputable culture collection in order to ensure reproducibility of the applied-for invention.

Where the United States led, patent practice in the United Kingdom and other European countries followed. The practice of depositing microorganisms for patent purposes is now widely recognized by patent offices in developed countries. It does not displace the legal requirement for as full and complete a description of the invention as the inventor can reasonably be expected to give, but it addresses the criticism that a patent could be issued on an application without anyone, other than the applicant or inventor, being able to perform the invention. The patent specification has to disclose when and where the deposit was made, and how the public can gain access to the deposit.

UPOV system of plant variety protection

Given the general view among plant breeders in the 1950s that the reproducibility requirement in patent law could not be met in the case of a new plant, it is not surprising that they should press for a different system to protect the work of the plant breeder. Their efforts in that regard led to the International Convention for the Protection of New Varieties of Plants

1961, otherwise known as the 'UPOV Convention'. The system established by the UPOV Convention avoids what was seen as the main obstacle to protection in the industrial patent system: it does not require the plant breeder to give a detailed taxonomic description, let alone a reproducible description, of the plant variety that he wants to protect. There are other important differences between the two systems, but these will not be discussed here.

Under the UPOV system, an applicant is required to submit reproductive material of the variety to the authority empowered by national law to grant protective rights. In the United Kingdom, under the Plant Varieties & Seeds Act 1964, the granting authority is the Plant Variety Rights Office, at Cambridge. The variety is grown by the granting authority, using this material, to see whether or not it complies with the criteria for a grant of such rights. If it is found to meet the criteria, the protective rights are granted. The granting authority produces a brief botanical description of the protected variety, but the ultimate reference is the reproductive material that justified the grant of the protective rights.

Description and disclosure

The rule relating to disclosure in modern patent systems usually runs, as, for example, in Article 83 of the European Patent Convention, that a patent applicant must 'disclose the invention in a manner sufficiently clear and complete for it to be carried out by a person skilled in the art'; and, as required in Article 84 EPC, the claims must be 'clear and concise and be supported by the description'. These rules are mirrored in the UK Patents Act 1977.

The description of an invention can be distinguished from its disclosure. A patent application may have a detailed taxonomic description of a newly invented plant, yet fail to disclose the plant invention adequately for patent purposes. On the other hand, a patent specification can be 'enabling' in the sense of patent law without lay people being able to comprehend the disclosure; or as the US Supreme Court put it in Webster Loom Company v Higgins in 1882: 'When an astronomer reports that a comet is to be seen with a telescope in the constellation of Auriga, in so many hours and minutes of right ascension, it is all Greek to the unskilled in science; but other astronomers will instantly direct their telescopes to the very point in the heavens where the stranger has made his entrance into our system. They understand the language of their brother scientist'. A patent specification is addressed to the person skilled in the pertinent art – who, in a given case, may be difficult to identify. That aside, a *real* skilled person in the relevant art, rather than the fictitious creature of patent law, may well find a patent specification almost as impenetrable as the lay person. The real skilled person, possessed of common general knowledge in the relevant art, is not necessarily educated to an appropriate standard in the written word as found in patent specifications. These tend to be tightly written, or in language incomprehensible to the real mechanic, electrician, or laboratory technician without a higher education. Patent law makes no allowance for this, but even where the skilled person is highly literate, in arts of the biological sciences, such as genetic engineering, he or she may also have to be qualified to a high technical standard in different scientific disciplines in order to comprehend the teaching of a patent specification. The fictional person of patent law (a somewhat dull, unimaginative knowall) may not be an individual but a team of persons of about PhD standard, including microbiologists experienced in such recombinant DNA techniques as those involved in gene cloning and probably, though not necessarily, a chemist skilled in the synthesis of biochemical compounds[4]. This virtually displaces the person skilled in the art with the 'person(s) expert in the art(s)' of the advanced biological sciences.

Describing a living invention

Under the UPOV system of plant variety, the living plant material represents the only true description of the variety. Taking this point further, it could be argued that a microorganism deposited for patent purposes is itself the only true description where the microorganism is the invention; that the deposit both describes and discloses the invention, and any detailed taxonomic description is superfluous. Should a patent applicant, where the invention is a microorganism or other living thing or material, be advised to give a full taxonomic description of the organism even where this may involve considerable research into its taxonomy? Or would it suffice for the applicant to describe the organism in a way acceptable to the art but insufficient according to the standards of a skilled taxonomist? There is no clear opinion on these questions in patent law. Caution would suggest, however, that a full taxonomic description be given where this is not already available in the taxonomic literature.

As sources of technical information, descriptions of living inventions, particularly microorganisms, in patent specifications should be viewed cautiously, and all the more so where the description has not been prepared by a taxonomist skilled in the species. This is not to suggest that taxonomy (also known as 'systematics') is an exact discipline: the taxonomy of microorganisms, for example, can be highly subjective, and controversial[5]. Classification may depend on whether the taxonomist is a 'lumper' or a 'splitter'[6]. Robbins wrote in 1960, that 'surrounding every species is a twilight area, where experts may disagree whether a given strain belongs to one species or another, this is not all. Within a species there can be many different strains comprising natural variations and induced mutants. Mutations can be induced artificially by many known techniques, such as X-ray and ultraviolet light treatment. Here also, it is extremely difficult to ascertain with certainty whether strains of the same species, which produce the same results, are actually the same or different. As distinguished from the scientific literature, the description of an alleged new organism in a patent specification has not usually been subjected to this screening process. The instinct of some inventors has been to baptize a newly discovered useful organism as a new species without 'benefit of clergy'[7]. There is no reason to believe that this remark is without some validity today.

Bacterial plasmids are used for cloning DNA. Given the accuracy of genetic engineering techniques, a repeatable disclosure for creating the cloning means can usually be given. However, this does not mean that the descriptions in patent specifications are problem-free. There is no uniform way of describing such plasmids[8]. Many modern specifications, for example US Patent 4 970 160 (issued 13 November 1990)[9] in respect of a gene for corn phosphoenolpyruvate carboxylase, give a nucleotide-by-nucleotide sequence of the patented gene, even though this is not yet a legal requirement. Another example of a nucleotide sequence can be found in the appendices to the decision of the Patents Court judgment on Genentech's HGH* patent (British Patent 2121048). It is a schematic diagram of the process in which the gene for somatostatin, made by chemical DNA synthesis, is fused to the *E.coli* beta-galactosidase gene on plasmid pBR322 (a well known recombinant cloning vehicle).

Standardizing descriptions of nucleotide sequences

The US Patent & Trademark Office (PTO) is trying to bring some order to the present diversity in descriptions. It is amending its regulations to establish a standardized format for descriptions of nucleotide and amino acid sequence data submitted as a part of patent applications, in conjunction with the required submission of these data in computer-readable form[10]. The reason for this amendment is to permit proper examination and processing of such applications, and to improve the quality and efficiency of the examination process, to promote conformity with usage of the scientific community, and to improve the dissemination of sequence

---

*   Human growth hormone

data in computer readable form. An example of an amino acid sequence is shown in Figure 12.1.

The current lack of uniformity in the submission of sequence data means that it is impractical for an examiner, searching a particularly lengthy sequence in a non-conforming format, accurately to key the query necessary to search the sequence by computer. Moreover, the lack of standardized symbols and a standardized format results in a very difficult comparison, both for the patent examiner and for the public, of what is claimed in a given patent application and what is disclosed in the prior art. Additionally, there is a risk that errors will arise when printing patent specifications involving lengthy and complex sequences. To facilitate compliance with the amended regulations, the US PTO will supply copies of the Authorin programs that have been tailored specifically to the patent requirements.

Written descriptions and novelty

If a written description of the invention of an animal, a plant, or a microorganism will not enable a person skilled in the art to replicate the teaching in a patent specification, then the description cannot destroy novelty by making the invention available to the public prior to filing for a patent. This point is well made by the American case In re LeGrice[11]. The plant breeder (LeGrice), resident in England, applied on 15 January 1958 for US patents on two varieties of rose. The applications were rejected by the US PTO on the ground that the varieties had been described in printed publications in England more than 1 year prior to filing for the patents. The publication, the *Rose Annual*, described the two roses, and certain catalogues had coloured pictures of them. LeGrice contested the PTO's rejection, arguing that the published information would not have enabled anyone to reproduce the plants. The appeal court accepted that argument, noting that 'Current studies to 'break the chromosome code' may also add to the knowledge of plant breeders so that they may some day secure possession of a plant invention by a description in a printed publication as is now possible in other fields of inventive effort'.

Value of disclosure after patent term

The patent system is a vast library of technical documents, accumulated over several hundred years. A disclosure in a patent specification for a mechanical or an electrical device, or a chemical compound, does not become any less 'enabling' with the passage of time, but the same cannot be said where the patent is for the invention of a new animal, plant or

(21) Int. Application Number:	PCT/JP89/00811	(51) International Patent Classification⁴ :	(11) Int. Publication Number:	WO 90/01542
(22) Int. Filing Date:	9 August 1989 (09.08.89)	C12N 9/02, 15/00	A1	
			(43) Int. Publication Date:	22 February 1990 (22.02.90)

(30) Priority data:
63/199295   9 August 1988   JP
                       (09.08.88)
63/204173   17 August 1988   JP
                       (17.08.88)

(71) Applicant *(for all designated States except US):* TORAY INDUSTRIES, INC. [JP/JP]; 2-1, Nihonbashi Muromachi 2-chome, Chuo-ku, Tokyo 103 (JP).

(72) Inventors; and
(75) Inventors/Applicants *(for US only)* : KAZAMI, Jun [JP/JP]; 1-20, Tsunishi 2-chome, Kamakura-shi, Kanagawa 248 (JP). NAKAMURA, Haruji [JP/JP]; 11-27, Miyamatsu-cho, Hiratsuka-shi, Kanagawa 254 (JP). GOTO, Toshio [JP/JP]; 3-9, Yaguma 1-chome, Nakagawa-ku, Nagoya-shi, Aichi 454 (JP).

(81) Designated States: AT (European patent), BE (European patent), CH (European patent), DE (European patent), FR (European patent), GB (European patent), IT (European patent), JP, KR, LU (European patent), NL (European patent), SE (European patent), US.

Published
With international search report.

(54) Title: LUCIFERASE, LUCIFERASE-CODING GENE, AND PROCESS FOR PREPARING LU-CIFERASE

(57) Abstract

Luciferase having the amino acid sequence of Fig. 1 and a gene coding it are disclosed. In addition, a recombinant vector DNA wherein the luciferase-coding gene is connected to the downstream portion of a promoter capable of expressing in each host cell, a transformant obtained by transforming each host cell by the vector DNA, and a process for preparing luciferase using such transformants are also disclosed.

Figure 12.1   Example of an abstract giving an amino acid sequence (with acknowledgements to WIPO)

microorganism. A deposit of biological material supplements a patent specification that, without a deposit, may not disclose the invention properly or adequately. However, there is no obligation on a patent holder, following expiry of his patent, to maintain (and ensure public availability of) an appropriate sample or culture of the organism or representative biological material, in perpetuity. It may be that samples already made available to the public will be maintained in a viable condition for future use, yet the general record on the conservation of genetic resources is not promising. On the contrary, biological resources are under constant threat in various parts of the world.

References

1. An anonymous note entitled 'Les brevets pour nouvautés végétales' in *La Propriete Industrielle*, January 1933, pages 22–23, gave this view (which was repeated many times, and for many years, thereafter): 'A level is always a level; a rotating shaft is always a rotating shaft and even a complex chemical compound always maintains the same molecular structure. On the other hand, as conditions change, plants also change... The result is that a verbal description, or even well prepared coloured plates, are not sufficient when it is necessary to define a new plant variety with the required accuracy... The courts will have to attenuate yet further the rigidity of the principle that the inventor, in exchange for the rights afforded him, must reveal his invention to society in such a way that any person 'skilled in the art' may carry it out; apply in a broad sense the theory which considers the products of nature as excluded from patentability... In fact, it would seem that even if the law represents good seed, case law will have to prove that it is not unfertile ground'.

2. The Engholm Committee, when it considered in its *Report on Plant Breeders' Rights* (Cmnd 1092, July 1961, HMSO) using the British patent system to protect new plant varieties, referred as follows to the problem of disclosure: 'In the case of living plants, such a system could not work in the same way as for methods of manufacture. Fundamentally, a plant is a self-reproducing mechanism. When the breeder has completed his work on a new variety, it is usually possible for others to multiply and use it without necessarily knowing how it was bred ... Even if the method could be fully described and published, the information would seldom be of any help to other people who might wish to attempt to recreate the variety from the breeder's starting material. Moreover a written description of the variety itself, giving details of its characteristics and behaviour, often is not precise enough to

identify the variety conclusively. Such descriptions are useful, but plant material is too variable, and varieties in many cases too similar, for a plant breeders' rights system to depend solely on written documents. Disputes about identity can only be settled finally by reference to the plants themselves'.

3. In *American Cyanamid Co v Upjohn Co* [1970] 3 All ER 785, Lord Wilberforce commented: 'Strains of microorganisms have been found to be useful in various connections; but very large numbers of differing varieties are found in nature. The problem for the scientist lies in identifying and isolating the particular strains of which, or mutants of which, use can be made. These may come to light by painstaking or expensive research assisted by good fortune or pure good fortune; once identified they represent a valuable asset. It may take many years of search for other scientists, however competent, and although provided with full information as to the characteristics of the strain, to isolate the same strain for themselves, if indeed they can ever succeed in doing so. In order to preserve useful strains and to make them available for use, there have been established culture collections where samples can be deposited'.

4. See, for example, *Genentech Incorporated's (Human Growth Hormone) Patent* [1989] RPC 613.

5. See Whittenberg, Microbiological Patents In International Litigation, 13 *Advances in Applied Microbiology* **383** (1969). Eisenschitz and Thompson, Descriptions of Microorganisms in Patents and Journal Articles, 4 *World Patent Information* **126** (1982), may be adverting to this when they write: 'Detailed information on a new microorganism will also be of interest to the biologists who see to their classification and it is important that the details are published in a recognized journal for validation by the whole community. Otherwise the classification scheme will become disorganized'. Goodier writes thus, on conventional taxonomy 'The basic unit is the species and there is a vast literature on what a species is and how it is defined... One approach is to choose a standard – the type specimen – and collect all the samples that match that specimen. When an organism is found that does not match any existing standard then it becomes a new type. The other approach is to identify some biological connection such as shared ecology or reproductive strategy... However good these methods are they all consist of dividing up nature into groups. There is at least a hint of arbitrariness about this' (from an unpublished PhD thesis, Department of Information Science, The City University, London).

6. Waksman wrote in 1957, at 21 *Bact. Rev.* 1, that 'many new

species have been described recently, largely because it is easier to create a new species that to attempt to correlate the characteristics of a freshly isolated culture with those of a known species already described in the literature, The problem has become particularly acute when Company A, for example, presents claims that to produce the same antibiotic it is using a different species than that claimed in the patent granted to Company B.'

7. Patents for Microbiological Transformations. *Journal of the Patent Office Society*, (1960), Volume **XLII**, p. 830

8. But see Novick, Uniform Nomenclature for Bacterial Plasmids: A Proposal, 40 *Bact. Rev.* 168 (1976).

9. Information scientists in the United Kingdom who want a copy of this particular specification, and any other patent specification relating to the life sciences, should contact the Science Reference and Information Service, British Library, London (telephone: 071-323 7916).

10. See *Federal Register*, Volume 35, Number 84, Tuesday 1 May 1990, 18230 et seq.

11. *Federal Reports*, 2nd series, 1962, v 301, p 929 (Court of Customs and Patent Appeals)

CHAPTER THIRTEEN

Future developments and further reading

Overview

Looking back over the centuries-long history of patents, it is striking how the 1970s, particularly in Europe, have turned out to be one of the decades of greatest activity. The chronology runs:

1970	conclusion of the Patent Cooperation Treaty
1971	Strasbourg Agreement on the International Patent Classification
1972	establishment of INPADOC
1973	conclusion of the European Patent Convention
1975	publication of the Community Patent Convention
1977	major revision of British patent law
1978	first European Patent applications filed

To these specific events may be added the rapid development of online databases, which in the 1970s really began to make a serious impact on the library and information scene. By 1980 there were already about 400 separate databases of all types; today the figure is in excess of 4500, of which a significant number relate exclusively to intellectual property.

The 1990s, emerges as a period of assimilation and consolidation in which the demand for information from patents shows no sign of slackening, and in which the means for obtaining patent information and the awareness of its value are greatly increased.

The major event which does not fit neatly into the above chronology is the 1961 International Convention for the Protection of New Varieties of Plants (the UPOV Convention), an issue the public awareness of which is increasing as more and more horticultural and gardening catalogues caution customers about the need to respect plant breeders' rights. The UPOV Convention was discussed in Chapter 12.

Looking ahead, three separate issues stand out as being of particular importance, meriting a closer look: firstly, patents as a measure of national and industrial-sector inventiveness, especially in the light of the trend away from national routes; secondly, the impact of CD-ROM technology on patent storage and searching routines; and lastly, the continuing public interest in and fascination with patents in general. Each issue is considered in turn.

Measures of national inventiveness.

Applications for patents are frequently used as a measure of a country's industrial health and entrepreneurial spirit, and it is possible to make qualified statistical comparisons between the leading industrially developed nations. In the case of Great Britain, a number of recent studies make the point that the level of innovation appears to be falling off. For example, the appraisal by Bain and Co.[1], already referred to in Chapter 10, which was presented at a conference organized by Business in the Community on behalf of the Prince of Wales Award for Innovation, revealed that, using European patent registrations as a proxy for inventive activity, the United Kingdom falls behind the United States, the Federal Republic of Germany, Japan and France in the absolute number of applications filed. On a per capita basis, that is, the number of patents per million of population, the United Kingdom lies in fourth place, just ahead of the United States. Clearly however there are some special cultural and educational influences at work, for whilst Germany is credited with around 200 applications per million population, the figures for the other countries in the comparison fit into a band of between 60 and 90 applications per million inhabitants.

Part of the magnitude of the German figure may be accounted for by the incentive embodied in that section of German patent law which requires financial compensation to be paid to employee inventors whose patents are commercially exploited and make a contribution to a company's revenue. The system is necessarily elaborate, with the need to keep extensive sales records and to hold regular appraisal meetings to ensure fair play both for the inventors and the company. Amounts for payments are calculated in very small fractions of a percent, but nevertheless, in the case of mass-produced articles featuring an employee's invention, can soon build up considerable sums.

Such a formal structure has not been adopted in Great Britain, where the view is taken that inventions produced in the course of an employee's normal duties belong to the employer. There is, however, a provision in the 1977 Act for some financial recognition in the case of employee inventors whose ideas prove to be of outstanding benefit to an organization. The difficult question of what is meant by the term 'outstanding benefit' is one likely to be resolved by case law.

Another set of findings, based on a similar approach, is contained in the 1990 *Annual Review of Government Funded Research and Development*[2], which notes that Great Britain is the only country to record a fall in the number of patents taken out in the United States. The level, again measured on a per capita basis, dropped from 44.37 per million people in the period 1963–1968 to 44.06 per million in the 5 years 1984–1988, a real decline of 0.13%. In so doing, Britain's position fell from second to last. The *Review* also reflected that there is a significant relationship between the per capita expenditure on industrial research and development and the volume of patenting activity.

However, a fall in inventiveness cannot be the only reason to account for a drop in filings. The British Technology Group, a body with a prominent record in the encouragement of innovation, and the publisher of such booklets as *Help the inventor*, warned at the 1990 annual meeting of the British Association for the Advancement of Science[3] that more than half the patent applications made on behalf of British universities and research councils are abandoned midway. Even when exploitation is successful, the Group maintains, the patent will be infringed, probably in the United States, where to take an infringer to court requires a minimum of £1 million commitment, and may cost many times more.

Certainly, patent cases in the United States courts can take a very long time to resolve, as evidenced for example by the inventor Gilbert Hyatt in his efforts to challenge the Intel Corporation over the ownership of the rights to the microchip.[4] Another enduring battle for recognition and compensation has been that of R.W. Kearns,[5] inventor of an intermittent-wipe mechanism for vehicle windscreens.

In considering patents as a measure of national inventiveness, it is worth noting that similar studies can be undertaken at a company or an industry level, where attempts are sometimes made to correlate commercial success with the numbers of patents being filed by employees. Even here, however, care must be exercised in making judgements for quite apart from the qualitative aspects as distinct from the quantitative ones, many progressive companies prefer not to be pioneers, and instead choose licensing agreements rather than their own filings as a reliable method of establishing and maintaining a technical lead.

Campaigns to encourage inventiveness and to remind private inventors in particular to protect their ideas, in order to reap some financial reward, are undertaken from time to time but again, great care is required, as the British Patent Office found out when it ran an advertisement featuring a picture of a radio with the caption 'No FM patent – no financial benefit'. A technical journalist pointed out that the FM radio had been patented by the American Edwin Armstrong in 1933. By the time of his death in 1954 he had received royalties of almost $5 million.[6]

Improved searching facilities

As noted elsewhere in this book, more and more patents files are being made available as CD-ROM publications, and the future expansion of this form of distribution will depend on the extent of user take-up, since the medium seems to be a beneficiary of technology push as much as market pull.

By way of explanation, CD-ROM (Compact Disc – Read Only Memory) is a high-storage capacity optical disc, 4.75 inches in diameter and weighing only one-sixtieth of an ounce. It is made of durable plastic with a reflective metal coating and lacquered surface, and is capable of storing 660 megabytes of data – the equivalent of 330 000 typewritten pages. Searching is carried out on an MS-DOS AT-compatible computer, with suitable software, usually available from the CD-ROM suppliers. One can use a network system to access CD-ROMs, an arrangement which has the advantage of multiuse, with more than one person being able to access the data at the same time. Again, suitable advice on setting up networks can be obtained from CD-ROM suppliers. No online costs are incurred in using CD-ROM, but the following financial aspects need to be taken into consideration:

1. Start-up costs

2. Purchase costs (often by means of an annual subscription)

3. Licence fees, which may be payable to certain producers,particularly with networking.

The role of CD-ROM has been called into question by those who ask whether it is in fact a transient technology,[7] whilst others have been quick to state that the medium is here to stay.[8] A comparison of one Europe-wide and two major British surveys on the use of CD-ROM and other optical products in academic, government, public and special libraries[9] made no reference at all to the use of patent databases. Taking the aggregate of the three surveys, the most popular CD-ROM proved to be MEDLINE (all versions), followed by the Books in Print databases.

Criticisms of CD-ROM include a slow speed of retrieval compared with advanced PC technology, limited capacity of the disks, and a range of differences in search commands. CD-ROM technology may not be transient, but it has a considerable way to go to gain general acceptance in the industrial property field. Nevertheless a number of organizations have announced the availability of CD-ROM files, including the European Patent Office, Research Publications, SilverPlatter and MicroPatent.

The service from the European Patent Office is called ESPACE, and embraces four series, namely ESPACE-FIRST giving the front pages of all PCT and EPO applications, including abstracts and drawings where available, and ESPACE-EP, ESPACE-WORLD and ESPACE-UK, providing, respectively, complete facsimiles in the original format of EP applications, PCT applications and UK 'A' documents.

Research Publications offer OG/PLUS and PATENT HISTORY on CD-ROM. The former is full-text image, abstracts, status data and litigation activity information derived weekly from the *US Patent and Trademark Office Gazette*, whilst the latter is a compilation of data partially originating in Patent Status File and LitAlert, providing the complete history of all active US patents.

SilverPlatter makes available parts of the general database CLAIMS, compiled by the IFI/Plenum Data Corporation as CLAIMS/Patent CD, giving access to over 1.8 million patents issued from the US Office since 1950.

MicroPatent, a joint venture between Opus Publications Inc. and Chadwyck-Healey, has launched APS (Automated Patent Searching), giving abstracts and bibliographic data on United States patents in CD-ROM format, with back-files to 1975.

The suggestion noted above that CD-ROM may be merely a transient technology is borne out by the announcement of new media such as CD-I (Compact Disc Interactive), a standard for a fully interactive system under development by Philips and Sony, which will provide for the handling of music, speech, still pictures, graphics, computer programs and computer data. Potential areas of CD-I include:

- Entertainment
- Education 'Edutainment' (learning through entertainment)
- Training
- In-car navigation
- Reference works
- Home shopping

Many of the initial products are likely to be in the form of sophisticated electronic encyclopaedias and reference books. CD-I is particularly attractive for databases concerned with patents, because it offers immense capacity for the storage of full specification texts, complete with drawings and diagrams.

Continuing general interest

Each year many articles are published pointing out just how useful patents can prove to be, not only to specialists such as information workers, scientists and technologists, but also to businessmen and industrialists.[10, 11, 12, 13] In addition, some attempts are made to survey developments in key technical areas as reflected by both patents and non-patent literature. A good example is the volume in the *European Patent Office Applied Technology* series, which looks at industrial robots[14] in terms of their design features and areas of application. Other topics in the same series to receive similar treatment include optical fibres, solid state video cameras, and microprocessors.

Some authors choose to draw attention to examples of developments which could not be followed through a study of the conventional literature because they concern unconventional ideas. A typical example is a recent paper on what are termed 'odd automotive inventions'.[15] Such articles make good copy, but it should be borne in mind that they are written with the benefit of hindsight and overlook the fact that the significance (or lack of it) of an invention may not have been appreciated at the time of its disclosure as a patent application.

Public interest is also stimulated and maintained when patented inventions receive some form of national recognition. Thus the idea described in the item 'Pure genius?' in the Winter 1989 issue of *Patents Information News* on how draught Guinness could be canned for home use without losing its distinctive creamy texture[16] received further widespread publicity when it was announced in April 1991 that the Guinness Company, owners of the patent, had received a Queen's Award for Industry in the technology category.

Many people would argue that inventions, no matter how unlikely or impractical they may seem at the time of announcement, need to be taken seriously if there is the remotest chance they may work, for they just might undermine existing market positions and threaten established product ranges. Thus in the late 1950s, an announcement that thermoelectricity using the Peltier effect had been harnessed in the Soviet Union for the powering of portable radios, led to an intensive spate of defensive research on thermoelectric devices in general, with particular regard to the application of exhaust heat from internal combustion engines. The view was taken that such a concept might offer a real alternative to existing means of generating electricity in vehicles, namely dynamos and alternators. In the event the threat proved unfounded.

The general point worth repeating is that, as with many other forms of publication, the information contained in patents is largely of an unspectacular nature, building steadily on the orthodoxy of what has gone before.

Finally, and as a tailpiece on the question of public interest, it seems that old myths die very hard. The story of the everlasting electric light bulb (a variant of the everlasting match) being invented, patented and then suppressed, continues to crop up. A correspondent was moved to ask a *Notes and Queries*[17], column 'Could somebody confirm or scotch for all time that enduring rumour concerning everlasting light bulbs, the patent of which was supposedly bought by an unscrupulous manufacturer so that they could never be produced'. Six different answers were provided, but whether the rumour has been scotched 'for all time' is most unlikely.

Further reading

Quite apart from the many works which touch upon the human interest aspects of patents, ranging from Dickens' Poor man's tale of a patent (*Household Words* 19 October 1850) to the account of the dogged struggle of Ron Hickman, inventor of the Workmate, there are several excellent reference books which are regularly reissued or updated to deal with the latest legal and procedural aspects of industrial property. In addition, there are numerous texts dealing with various specific matters relating to patents, extending from sources of information to aids for inventors. Just a selection of such titles is given below.

Blanco White, T.A. (1983) *Patents for inventions and the protection of industrial designs*. London: Stevens & Sons

Blanco White, T.A., Jacob, R. and Davies, J D. (1986) *Patents, trade marks, copyright and industrial designs*. London: Sweet & Maxwell

Chisum, D.S. (1990) *Patents – a treatise on the law of patentability validity and infringement*. New York: Matthew Bender

Dworkin, G. and Taylor, R.D. (1989) *Blackstone's guide to the Copyright Designs and Patents Act 1988*. London: Blackstone Press

Eisenschitz, T.S. (1987) *Patents, trade marks and designs in information work*. London: Croom Helm

Eisenschitz, T.S. and Phillips, J. (1985) *The inventor's information guide*. London: Intellectual Property Law Unit, Queen Mary College

Encyclopedia of United Kingdom and European Patent law (1990) London: Sweet & Maxwell; W Green & Son.

Grubb, P.W. (1986) *Patents in chemistry and biotechnology*. Oxford: Clarendon Press

Haynes, D., editor (1990) *Information sources in information technology*. London: Bowker-Saur

Hill, M. (1979) *Patent documentation* Derived from a German edition by A. Wittmann and R. Schiffels. London: Sweet & Maxwell

Katzarov, K. (1990) *Katzarov's manual on industrial property all over the world*. 10th edn. Geneva: Katzarov SA, 10th edition.

Konold, W.G. *et al.* (1979) *What every engineer should know about patents.* New York: Dekker

Phillips, J. (ed) (1985) *Patents in perspective.* Oxford: ESC Publishing Ltd. (See especially Ch.5 Value of patent information, by T.S. Eisenschitz, pp. 42-53; and Ch.6 Information aspects of patents, by C. Oppenheim, pp. 54–67.).

Rimmer, B.M. (1988) *International guide to official industrial property publications*, 2nd edn. London: British Library, with 1990 update

Rimmer, B.M. (1988) *Patent information and documentation in Western Europe: an inventory of services available to the public*, 3rd edn. London: K.G.Saur

Rosenberg, P.D. (1990) Patent law fundamentals, 2nd edition. New York: Clark Boardman

Schade, H. (1980) *Patents at a glance – a survey of substantive law and formalities in 50 countries*, 3rd edn. Cologne: Carl Heymanns Verlag

Seemann, R.A. (1987) *Patent smart – a complete guide to developing, protecting and selling your invention.* Englewood Cliffs: Prentice-Hall

Shaw, L. (1982) *Patents, designs, copyright, trade marks – the practical guide for people with a new idea.* Birmingham: Laurence Shaw. (Revised edition 1990, published by the Patent Eye, Bilgrey Samson Information Services, Birmingham.)

Van Dulken, S. (ed) (1990) *Introduction to patents information.* London: British Library, Science Reference & Information Service

Williams, J.F. (1986) *A manager's guide to patents, trademarks and copyright.* London: Kogan Page

The above list excludes the many guides for inventors and similar publications mentioned elsewhere in the text and issued directly from various patenting authorities around the world. Some, like the booklet *Patents: a source of technical information*, prepared by the British Patent Office, are obtainable free of charge on request; others, such as *General information concerning patents*, from the US Patent and Trademark Office, are available on payment of a small fee. Such documents are normally written with the general reader in mind, and are subject to regular revision – the latest details about current titles are best obtained from the appropriate offices listed in the appendix.

References

1   Bain and Co. (1990) *Innovation in Britain today: how major companies can help innovation – and themselves.* London: Bain and Co.

2   *Annual review of Government R&D* (1990). London: Her Majesty's Stationery Office

3 Exploitation is a two-way street (1990). *Daily Telegraph*, 28 September
4 Pioneer with a microchip on his shoulder (1990). *Guardian*, 27 November
5 Thomas, C.M. (1989) Inventor of the blinking wipe to have his day in court. *Automotive News*, September 18, p. 3 (R.W. Kearns v. Ford)
6 Patently wrong (1991) *Observer*, 17 February
7 McSean, T. and Law, D. (1990) Is CD-ROM a transient technology? *Library Association Record*, **92** (11) 837-838, 841
8 Brewerton, A.W. (1990) We should be praising CD-ROM, not burying it. *Library Association Record*, **92** (12) 909
9 Raitt, D.I. and Chen, C-c. (1990) Optical product take-up in UK libraries: a comparison of some recent studies. *Library Association Record*, **92** (12) 924, 926–927
10 Perry, N.J. (1986) The surprising new power of patents. *Fortune*, **115**, June 57-63
11 Willis, C. (1988) It pays to patent. *Venture*, 10 October 38–39
12 Alster, N. (1988) New profits from patents. *Fortune*, **117**, April 25, 185-186 *et seq.*
13 Harbert, T. (1990) Patent portfolios emerge as corporate money makers. *Electronic Business*, 16, April **16**, 53–54 *et seq.*
14 Lammineur, P. and Cornillie, O. (1984) *Industrial robots.* Oxford: Pergamon Press (EPO Applied Technology Series, vol. 2)
15 Baumann, R. (1988) Patently bizarre – not all great ideas bear fruit (odd automotive inventions that have received US patents). *Wards Automotive World*, **24**, March, 59–60
16 Forage, A. and Byrne, W. (1987) *Carbonated beverage container.* GB 2183592 (Priority 1985)
17 *Notes and Queries* (1991) *Guardian*, 18 & 25 February.
18 See for instance Hickman, R.P. and Roos, M.J. Workmate. *Journal of the Chartered Institute of Patents Agents*, **11**, (10), 426-457

APPENDIX ONE

Glossary

Abridgment a summary of the disclosure of a patent specification, formerly written by the UK Patent Office examiner

Abstract a summary of the disclosure of a patent specification, written
by the applicant

Acceptance the formal decision by the UK Patent Office that a patent
should be granted

Allowance the US term for acceptance

Amendment an alteration made to a patent specification during prosecution or after grant

Anticipation the prior art which destroys the novelty of a claim by fully
describing something falling within it

Best mode requirement in the United States, the obligation to describe
the best way of carrying out the invention

Characterizing clause that part of a German or European style claim
which indicates the novel features of the invention

Claim the part of a specification which defines the the scope of protection

Classmark a combination of letters and numbers which indicates a heading within a patent classification system

Continuation-in-part application in the US, a new filing of a specification with alterations or additions to the specification

Convention country a state which is a member of the Paris Convention
for the Protection of Industrial Property

Convention year a period of 12 months from a first application in a convention country, within which applications having the effective date of
the original filing may be filed in other convention countries

Defensive patent a patent which does not cover fully what the patentee is doing, but which helps to keep competitors away from the area of interest

Deferred examination a system in which the examination of a patent application may be postponed for several years until requested by the applicant

Designation the naming of countries for which a European or PCT application is being filed

Early publication the publication of an application before examination

Exhaustion of rights the principle that when patented goods have been sold by the patentee, he has no further control over them

File history in the US, the dossier containing all papers relevant to the prosecution of an application; also called the **File wrapper**

Generic claim a claim which covers a number of compounds defined by common structural features

Grace period a period of time before the filing date of an application, during which certain types of publication do not invalidate the application

In-convention filing a filing made in a foreign country within 12 months of the original home filing, treated under the Paris Convention as having a priority date as of the original filing

Infringement the act of doing something forbidden by the grant of a patent to another

Insufficiency a ground of invalidity of a patent if the description does not enable the reader to work the invention

Know how unpatented technical or commercial information

Licence of right an endorsement on a patent to the effect that anyone may have a licence upon reasonable terms

Man skilled in the art the hypothetical person to whom the patent specification is addressed

Markush group a group of compounds or substituents defined for the purpose of a patent claim and lacking a common generic description

Non-convention filing *see* **Out-of-convention filing**

Novelty the essential condition for patentability, that what is claimed is new

Obvious capable of being performed by the average skilled man in possession of the prior art

Official action (US), **Official letter** (UK) communications from the Patent Office examiner raising objections to a patent application

Omnibus claim a claim claiming the invention as described with reference to the drawing or examples

Opposition proceedings before a Patent Office in which a third party raises objections to the grant of a patent

Out of convention filing a foreign filing made more than 12 months after the original home filing, and so unable under the terms of the Paris Convention to claim the original priority date

Precharacterizing clause a part of a German or European style claim which recites the features of the invention which are already known

Prior art all publications before the priority date which could be relevant to the novelty or unobviousness of an invention

Prior use the use of an invention before the priority date of an application claiming it

Priority date the date on which an invention was first disclosed to a patent office in the application in question, or in an earlier application from which it validly claims priority

Provisional specification in the UK, formerly a brief description of the invention filed with an application, to be followed by the complete specification

Renewal fee a fee payable at intervals to a patent office to maintain a granted patent in force

Restoration proceedings to revive a patent which has lapsed due to non-payment of renewal fees

Scope the total field encompassed by a patent claim

Specification the description of an invention filed with a patent application

State of the art the total information in the relevant field known to the hypothetical man skilled in the art

Substantive examination examination by a patent office examiner for patentability, as distinct from purely formal matters

Term the lifetime of a patent (20 years in most countries)

Working requirements provisions that a patent will be subject to compulsory licensing or lapse unless the invention is operated commercially in the country in question

APPENDIX TWO

List of organizations mentioned in the text

Association of the British Pharmaceutical Industry (ABPI)
12 Whitehall
London SW1A 2DY

Australian Patent
Trade Marks and Designs Offices
PO Box 200
Woden
ACT
2606 Australia

Automobile Association
Fanum House
Basingstoke
Hants RG21 2EA

Bain and Co.
16 Connaught Place
London W2 2ES

Birmingham Patents Library
Science and Technology
Department
Chamberlain Square
Birmingham B3 3HQ

British Library
Science Reference and
Information
Service (SRIS) and Japanese
Information Service (JIS)
25 Southampton Buildings
London WC2A

British Technology Group
101 Newington Causeway
London SE1 6BU

Carlo Biscaretti di Ruffia Motor
Museum
40 Corso Unita d'Italia
Turin
Italy

Chartered Institute of Patent
Agents (CIPA)
Staple Inn Buildings
London WC1V 7PZ

Chemical Abstracts Service
PO Box 3012
Columbus
Ohio 43210
USA

Commission of the European
Communities
Jean Monnet House
8 Storey's Gate
London SW1P 3AT

Current Patents Ltd
34–42 Cleveland Street
London W1P 5FB

Data-Star
DS Marketing Ltd
Plaza Suite
114 Jermyn Street
London SW1Y 6HJ

Department of Health
Richmond House
79 Whitehall
London SWIA 2NS
(The Department of Health was
formed in July 1988 by the division of the Department of Health
and Social Security (DHSS) into
two departments.)

Derwent Publications Ltd
Rochdale House
128 Theobalds Road
London WC1X 8RP

Deutsches Patentamt
Zweibruckenstrasse 12
D-8000 Munich 2
Germany

DIALOG
Learned Information/Dialog
PO Box 188
Oxford OXI 5AX

Dialtech *see* IRS-Dialtech

Engineering Index
Engineering Information Inc
345 East 47th Street
New York NY 10017
USA

ESPACE *see* European Patent Office

European Patent Office
Erhardtstrasse 27
D-8000 Munich 2
Germany

Food and Drug Administration
(FDA) Health and Human
Services Department
5600 Fishers Lane
Rockville MD 20857
USA

General Agreement on Tariffs
and Trade (GATT)
Centre William Rappard
154 rue de Lausanne
CH-1211 Geneva 21
Switzerland

Carl Heymanns Verlag KG
Luxemburgerstrasse 449
Postfach 410446
D-5000 Cologne 41
Germany

Infotap
2 rue A Borschette
BP 262
L-2012 Luxembourg

Institut National de la Propriété
Industrielle (INPI)
26bis rue de Leningrad
75800 Paris
Cedex 08
France

Institute of Patentees and Inventors
Suite 505A
189 Regent Street
London W1R 7WF

Intelligent Information *see* Infotap

International Patent Documentation Centre (INPADOC)
Moellwaldplatz 4
A-1041 Vienna
Austria

International Translations Centre (ITC)
Scuttersveld 2
2611 W E Delft
Netherlands

IRS-Dialtech
Science Reference and Information Service
25 Southampton Buildings
London WC2A 1AW

Japanese Information Service (JIS) see British Library

Japanese Patent Information Organisation (JAPIO)
3-4-2 Kasumigaseki
Chiyoda-ku
Tokyo
Japan

Japanese Patent Office
4-3 Kasumigaseki
3-Chome
Chiyoda-ku
Tokyo
Japan

Leeds City Libraries
Patents Information Unit
32 York Road
Leeds LS9 8TD

MicroPatent
25 Science Park
New Haven CT 06511
USA

National Technical Information Service (NTIS)
Springfield
VA 22161
USA

OPTI-NET
Optech Ltd
East Street
Farnham
Surrey GU9 7XX

ORBIT
Maxwell Online
Achilles House
Western Avenue
London W3 OVA

Organization for Economic Co-operation and Development (OECD)
2 rue Andre-Pascal
75116 Paris
France

Patent and Trademark Office (PTO) *see* United States Department of Commerce

Patentanwaltskammer
Postfach 26108
D-8000 Munich 26
Germany

Patent Office
Cardiff Road
Newport
Gwent NP9 1RH; London office
for the receipt of documents for
onward transmission to Newport:
25 Southampton Buildings
London, WC2A 1AY. (NB: State
House, 66–71 High Holborn, London WC1R 4TP ceased to be the
official address of the Patent Office after 28 April 1991.)

Patent Information Network (PIN)
Room 14
The British Library
25 Southampton Buildings
London WC2A 1AW

Plant Variety Rights Office
Ministry of Agriculture, Fisheries
& Food
White House Lane
Huntingdon Road
Cambridge CB3 OLF (The Office
publishes a journal, *Plant Var-
ieties and Seeds Gazette*)

Questel
Scientific Systems Ltd
London House
London Road South
Poyton
Cheshire SK12 1YP

Research Publications Inc
PO Box 45
Reading RG1 8HF

Science Abstracts
Inspec Marketing Department
PO Box 96 Stevenage
Herts SG1 2SD

Science Reference and Information Service (SRIS)
see British Library

SilverPlatter Information Inc
10 Barley Mow Passage
London W4 4PH

STN
Royal Society of Chemistry
Thomas Graham House
Science Park
Milton Road
Cambridge CB4 4WF

United States Department of Com-
merce
Patent and Trademark Office
(PTO)
Washington DC 20231
USA

Wila Verlag
Wilhelm Lampl KG
Landsbergerstrasse 191a
D-8000 Munich 21
Germany

World Intellectual Property Organization (WIPO)
34 chemin des Colombettes
CH-1211 Geneva 20
Switzerland

Index